Table of Co

~Acknowledgements~

I am most grateful to all of the citizens and leaders of my adopted home of Park City who've worked so hard to make this beloved town the pedestrian-friendly place it has come to be. Thanks are also extended to the friends and family who supported this endeavor, especially Kenneth Hurwitz M.D., Nancy Costo, Margie Hurwitz, Jodyne Roseman, and Audrey Siegel. I am also grateful for the assistance provided by reviewers David Hampshire, Mahala Ruddell, Sandra Morrison, and Rebecca Rauch, illustrator Matthew Rue, cartographer Tom Childs, and photography contributors Nick Calas, Basu Ghosh, Joseph Klimasiewfski, Jon Scarlet, and the unnamed photographers who are so generous as to contribute their prized photos to the public domain. All uncredited photos were taken by the author.

~Why Walk~

Park City's reputation as a haven for skiers, cyclists, hikers, shoppers and Sundance film lovers, overshadows the fact that it's a wonderful place to just go for a walk.

This book will guide you through a variety of routes along paved paths and roads in and around the cornucopia of neighborhoods that comprise this spectacular mountain community. Some easy off-road trails are included to whet appetites for hiking.

The walks herein will expose you to Park City's colorful history and diverse ecology. Hopefully, this book will also inspire you to become a walker. The benefits of walking are plentiful and profound.

CONSIDER THAT:

Walking is the most natural, **safest,** and most readily available form of human exercise.

Regular walking improves **fitness, health, weight control, sleep, mood,** and **longevity,** and is therapeutic for many diseases.

Walking improves **cognition**. Some of history's most revered thinkers, such as Plato, Aristotle, Nietzsche, and Thomas Jefferson were avid walkers, and are said to have done their best thinking while walking.

Walking is **free.**

You can walk almost **anywhere, anytime,** even if you only have a few minutes or are stuck in an airport.

Walkers can **get to places** where other travelers cannot go, not even on a bicycle.

No special equipment is needed. Your shoes won't be stolen while you stop for lunch. Your walking gear can be your everyday, everywhere gear.

Walking outdoors is a **sensory awakening**. A walker can see, hear, smell and touch things that motorists, cyclists and runners miss when they whiz by.

Regular walkers gain **appreciation of community** not experienced by other travelers. Many successful politicians start their careers by walking around their neighborhoods.

Success in business management and **leadership** may be more readily attained by walking around the workplace.

Walking with a friend or family member can **strengthen relationships.**

Walking can provide solitude or **private time** for those who need to de-stress, solve problems, make decisions, or get their creative juices percolating.

With discretion, walking can be **combined** with numerous other activities.

Imagine what a **healthier environment** you could live in if auto traffic was reduced because people embraced walking as transportation.

Your **kids** and **dogs** could benefit too.

You will be astounded by how **easy, invigorating, stimulating,** and **entertaining** walking can be. Alternatively, if you're seeking challenge, walking can be as hard as you care to make it.

~About Park City~

Just off Interstate Route 80 as it streams from New York City to San Francisco, the town of Park City sits on about 17.5 square miles (45.5 km²) of **mountain terrain 7,000 feet (2,133 m) above sea level.** Its official address is Summit County, Utah U.S.A.

The mountains of Park City are part of the **Wasatch Range** at the western edge of the **Rocky Mountains.** A few thousand feet shorter than the Colorado Rockies, the Wasatch stretch about 160 miles (257 km) from Idaho to central Utah. These mountains form the eastern edge of the **Great Basin** where an

Unlike remote mountain towns, Park City is readily accessible by an interstate highway and international airport.

ancient ocean formerly occupied the American southwest. The Great Salt Lake and Bonneville Salt Flats are remnants of that ocean.

Park City is said to be located along the **Wasatch Back,** while the Salt Lake Valley is often referred to as the Wasatch Front. It has been debated as to whether the name "Wasatch" in Native American language means "mountain pass," "low mountains," or "low place in high mountains".

The actual town of Park City, called **Old Town,** occupies a narrow canyon that spills out of the mountains from the even narrower Ontario and Empire Canyons. To the immediate west, south, and southeast are more mountains and canyons. To the north and northeast lies a mountain plateau that is occupied by Park City's suburbs and the **Snyderville Basin.**

Like other famous mountain resorts in the western United States, Park City developed in the middle of the 19th century as a mining town, and evolved into a ski town in the last half of the 20th century. In the face of burgeoning growth, Park City residents and their elected leaders have collaborated to preserve both the town's history and open space. Many Park City addresses are on historic registries and there are about **7,000 acres** of preserved **open space** and more than **400 miles (644+ km)** of maintained **trails** in and around the town. In fact, there are many more miles of trails than roads. There's also **free public bus service.**

The **2010 census** counted about 7,500 people living in approximately 2,900 households, with males outnumbering females by about 112 to 100. Approximately **70% of Park City residences are second homes** whose owners are not counted in the census. In 2015, about 4,800 students attended Park City's public schools and about 800 were enrolled in seven private schools and preschools.

Park City is one of the **wealthiest small towns** in America. Providing an easier commute to the state capital than do many locations along the Wasatch Front, it serves as a bedroom community for the rapidly growing Salt Lake City metropolis. Its easy access to an international airport is ideal for business travelers. In addition to tourism, retail, and service industries, several manufacturing companies, and farms and ranches in surrounding Summit and Wasatch Counties provide local employment. A research park is being developed in Kimball Junction.

The number of residents who live in Park City is greatly exceeded by the number of tourists that visit. Retirees from Arizona, Texas and other hot climates lease skier lodging in the summer. Salt Lake residents regularly come for skiing, concerts, and other activities and events, and to escape summer heat and winter inversions. It's estimated that Park City currently attracts more than **three million visitors** per year. Most come in winter but summer is almost as popular. Locals often say they moved here for winter, but they could never leave because summer is so fantastic. There are fewer visitors in spring and autumn, but no matter the season, many of the walks in this book can be enjoyed without crowds.

~Mountain Town Amenities~

While Park City's mountains are magnets for many, this tiny town also offers moun‐tains of eats, entertainment, education and enterprise.

EATS

Park City has about **180 restaurants** ranging from pricey fine dining on Main Street and at the resorts, to budget eateries in the suburbs. Seasonal **farmers' markets**, multiple supermarkets and boutique grocers, along with artisan bakers, cheese mongers, chocolatiers and other **food crafts** will delight cooks.

Although agriculture at altitude has its challenges, **community gardening** in Park City is "growing." Utah **ranchers** raise beef, hogs, lambs, dairy products, and chicken eggs. Utah **farmers** grow apples, cherries, peaches, raspberries, onions, po‐tatoes and dry beans. An **aquaculture** industry supplies the trout found on many local menus. Utah, nicknamed the "beehive state", is also known for its honey.

You can get a **drink in Utah**, but as in 17 other states, spirits by the bottle are sold only in state controlled liquor stores, which are closed on Sundays and holidays, including Pioneer Day, a state holiday on July 24. Grocery stores sell 3.2% beer but not wine or hard lemonade. Restaurants cannot serve alcohol unless food is pur‐chased, nor mix a cocktail in front of you. Don't blame the bartender; these are state laws. It's also illegal to transport or ship liquor from other states into Utah, but Park City does have its own brewery and distillery. Check laws at www.utah.com, state-liquor-laws.

Bear in mind that there is a **free transportation** system as well as driver services in Park City. You can party here and stay safe.

ENTERTAINMENT

Park City is a **live music** mecca. The nonprofit, Mountain Town Stages, sponsors 200+ concerts a year, and pro‐vides musician networking and school outreach pro‐grams. **Outdoor concerts** at the resorts, Newpark band shell, and other locations are often **free.** Check the website at www.mountaintownmusic.org/. **Nationally touring musicians** concerts are sponsored by the Park City Institute; website parkcity.institute.

Art is everywhere in Park City. Local painters and sculptures have decorated trails and tunnels, and some **30 galleries** feature imaginative creations and stunning images. The nonprofit Kimball Art Center, website kim‐ballartcenter.org/, sponsors exhibits, classes and work‐shops for artists, an annual arts festival, and special

Public pianos and sound gardens bring music and art together. Photo by Ken Hurwitz MD

A herd of artsy moose is on the loose in Park City. How many can you count?

events. Find **free gallery tours** at www.parkcitygallery-association.com/.

The Eccles Performing Arts Center at the Park City High School, and the Egyptian Theatre on Main Street host **live theater**, comedy, music, dance, and other presentations. Find schedules at ecclescenter.org/. and www.egyptiantheatrecompany.org/.

Live entertainment may also be found in restaurants, nightclubs, and other venues. The Park City Chamber of Commerce provides information at www.visitparkcity.com/.

Movie theaters are located at the Holiday Village Mall and in Redstone at Kimball Junction. **Select films** are screened at municipal facilities by www.parkcityfilmseries.com. During the **Sundance Film Festival**, big rooms all over town become movie-houses with bleacher seating. If you can find lodging during festival week, you may find that the gym or house of worship you planned to attend has been transformed into a temporary theater.

In addition to hosting Sundance, **Main Street** is also the venue for holiday parades, and special events. The **Silly Market** on summer Sundays features vendors and entertainment. Bike and running **races, food fests,** and nearby **rodeos** and **fairs** provide additional diversions.

Winter entertainment includes elite athlete and celebrity ski races, half-pipe competitions, sleigh rides, and dogsled rides and races. Spectators can also watch skiing **aerialists** train at the Utah Olympic Park year round.

Celebrity ties to Park City are legend. World leaders ski and politic here. Sometimes during the Sundance Film Festival, stargazers throng Main Street hoping to catch a glimpse of a luminary. At the local ice rink, I occasionally see children with bodyguards; bearing both the fruits and the pits of their parents' fame.

EDUCATION

Intriguing exhibits at the **Park City Museum** on Main Street capture the town's vibrant history and evolution. The website is parkcityhistory.org/.

The **Swaner Preserve** and **Ecocenter** provide a museum, environmental education, and guided tours. The website is: www.swanerecocenter.org/.

Find a **ski museum** at www.engenmuseum.org.

There's a **municipal library** in Old Town, a local branch of the **county library** in Kimball Junction, and various book exchange programs. Educational films, TED talks and similar offerings are sponsored by a number of local organizations.

In addition to highly rated public **schools**, private school options include an alternative high school for winter sports competitors. Park City has its own cooking and wine schools, as well as ski schools, fly-fishing schools, and just about any other kind of expert instruction you may be interested in.

ENTERPRISE

Lodging options range from opulent slope-side hotels and condos to dormitory facilities and an RV campground. Campsites are available in nearby state parks.

Park City has its own **newspaper** and **radio** and **TV stations**. The *Park Record* newspaper published twice weekly also provides on-line news at www.parkrecord.com/. KPCW, provides local news and programming on the radio dial at FM 91.7, and on-line at kpcw.org/. Television programming by PCTV can be found at parkcity.tv/.

Spas, gyms and **yoga** studios are prolific in Park City, with luxury hotels offering lavish facilities. There's a hospital, urgent care, and multiple private traditional and alternative medical practices. **High-end health care**, here in the home of the United States Ski and Snowboard Team, tends to attract elite and professional athletes.

Shopping in Park City is also an attraction. Main Street features stores not found anywhere else, and many merchants will package and ship purchases that won't fit in your suitcase. The Tanger outlets mall in Kimball Junction has continuously expanded. Consignment stores offer fabulous fashion and furnishings. Style devotees will feel right at home here, but so will those who tromp around in ski clothes or dusty denim.

Park City's residents and resorts support the development of wind and solar power, and a **picker's paradise** can be found at the local recycling center on Woodbine Way, website www.recycleutah.org/.

Park City **recreational opportunities** beyond skiing and snowboarding include: snowshoeing, snow tubing, snowmobiling, snow cycling (on bikes with snow tires), cycling, electric cycling, hiking, in-line skating, golf, tennis, pickleball, ice-skating, curling, hockey, bowling, horseback riding, swimming, stand-up paddle boarding, zip lining, mountain coasters and slides, ball fields and courts, skate and bike parks, and municipal and private gyms. There's also nearby fly-fishing, river running, sailing, rock climbing, and numerous national and state parks.

And finally, it's a **great place for walkers**. Park City and its surrounds are connected by an extensive trail system, a free public transportation system, and an aerial-transport system that makes magnificent mountain terrain accessible to all.

~Park City's Colorful Past~

Long before Park City was settled, **early humans** inhabited the Great Basin region of the southwest United States, starting around 13,000 years ago. The earliest people appear to have lived as nomadic hunters/gatherers in extended family groups. They followed herds of game and ripening plant resources, and produced tools made of bones, stones and wood.

From about AD 1 to AD 1300, the **Fremont Culture** thrived throughout most of Utah, north of the Colorado River. Unlike hunters and gatherers, these people depended on agriculture and lived in structures built partially into the ground (pit houses). They farmed corn, squash and beans, and made pottery and basketry. It's not known if the Fremont migrated due to drought, transitioned back to a hunter-gatherer existence, or blended with other tribes, but their unique cultural signature faded away after AD 1300.

Erratic weather with **droughts** and short growing seasons probably motivated migrations of early people. There is evidence of a 30-year drought in the southwest United States starting around AD 1270. About that time, Shoshonean (Numic) speaking people had come to occupy northern and eastern Utah. Their primary activities included hunting, gathering, and seasonal rounds of travel and trade. After **horses** and material goods were introduced to Native Americans by Spanish explorers in the late 1600s, the Shoshonean people became more mobile and expanded their terrain and trading routes. Ultimately, the Northern Shoshone, Goshute (Western Shoshone), Southern Paiute, and the Ute tribes came to call Utah home.

Utah **Native Americans** had a family-centered culture with great reverence for grandparents and women. They lived in groups of about 200 persons, scattered geographically to conserve game and plant food sources. Spanish colonial administrators didn't control the Shoshonean tribes like they did the Pueblo tribes to the south, but **intruders** started to change the way of life of local Native Americans in the 1820s, when the **Santa Fe Trail** from Missouri to New Mexico brought increasing numbers of trappers and traders north into Utah.

By the time the **Mormon pioneers** arrived in 1847, various tribes of Native Americans were living along the Wasatch Front. Conflict arose when Mormon settlements infringed on tribal farmland, fishing and hunting grounds. By the 1860s, a federal agent advised President Abraham Lincoln that the tribes had been driven into nakedness and famine, motivating these peaceful people to resort to raids and theft of livestock. In response, Utah's new settlers, who outnumbered the native people, demanded that the federal government intervene. (In 1830, Congress had passed the **Indian Removal Act**, empowering the U.S. government to forcibly remove Native Americans away from populations of European settlers.) Ultimately tribal lands were reduced to reservations, as shown on the map on page 8. Most Native Americans don't live on reservations, but Native Americans now comprise less than one percent of Summit County's population.

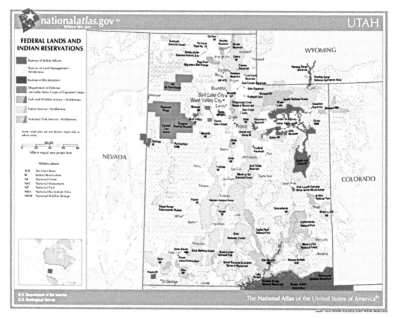

Pink shading represents federally designated tribal lands.
Source: U.S. Dept. of the Interior.

Park City's more **recent history** tells the story of a little 19th century mountain mining camp that became one of the best-loved resort destinations in the world.

In the **early 1800s** Native Americans, trappers and traders frequently traveled through the mountain pass that borders Park City. Mormon pioneers fleeing prejudice in Illinois, and on their way to settling Salt Lake City in 1847, brought their covered wagons through Emigration Canyon, a nearby pass through the Wasatch Mountains.

In 1848 entrepreneur **Parley P. Pratt** explored the canyon between Salt Lake City and the future Park City. Mormon leader **Brigham Young** gave Pratt the canyon, through which he promptly built a toll road in order to collect fees from travelers lured west by the **California Gold Rush** (1848-1855). This "Golden Pass" also provided a thoroughfare for stagecoaches and mail. Today Parley's Canyon is the byway of one of America's major roads, Interstate Route 80.

1850s: Utah lands were designated as an incorporated territory of the United States by an act of Congress in 1850. Utah wouldn't become the 45th state of the Union until 1896, after the Mormon practice of **polygamy** was renounced.

A few families migrated up Parley's Canyon in the early 1850s to **homestead** on the mountain plateau (basin) just north of future Park City. With its grassy meadows and abundant streams, the basin enabled the settlers to graze animals and grow food. Amongst the first settlers were **George** and **Rhoda Snyder**. There was also a **Samuel Comstock Snyder** who opened a lumber mill. The basin came to be called

Snyderville and "Snyder's Mill" is now one of its subdivisions.

1860s: William Kimball began operating a **stagecoach** through Parley's Canyon. Today **Kimball Junction** is the commercial center of the Snyderville Basin and a suburban extension of Park City.

During the **Civil War** (1861-1865), President Abraham Lincoln worried that Utah settlers might try to secede, as had Confederate States. He sent Union soldiers to monitor the settlers and protect federal mail routes. Some of these soldiers had been **prospectors** during the California Gold Rush and spent their leisure time looking for precious metals in the local mountains. Their searches lead to the discovery of rich veins of silver ore, as well as lead, zinc and gold.

News of the finds traveled fast, seducing adventurers from diverse backgrounds to come to Park City to seek their fortunes. At the same time, Mormon leader Brigham Young spurned the lure of precious metals and forbade his followers to prospect for any commodity other than coal. Young's plan for economic growth was agriculture. The small town of **Coalville**, settled by Mormon coal prospectors 25 miles to the north, was designated as the seat of county government to "rule over" the unruly mining camp to its south. Today, Park City's neighborhoods with names like Silver Springs, Silver Creek, Silver Summit, etc., commemorate the importance of **silver** to the area.

1870s: First settlers George and Rhoda Snyder named the area Parley's Park City. With its name quickly abbreviated, the town of Park City was born into America's **Gilded Age**. American author Mark Twain termed the period from the 1870s to about 1900 the "Gilded Age", because there seemed to be a thin golden veneer (gilding) covering over a morass of social problems and injustice. In Park City, the mines would ultimately create 23 millionaire owners, while legions of laborers toiled in cold, wet, dark, poorly ventilated tunnels with rocks falling on their heads, while inhaling mold and toxic dust, for ten hours every day except Independence Day and Christmas.

The states of America became "United" upon the end of the Civil War, and with the completion of the **Transcontinental Railroad** in 1869. Railroad construction required the labor of thousands of strong backs, but the Civil War had killed and maimed many young men and there was a nationwide shortage of workers, especially in the sparsely populated west. The need for laborers, and the fact that skilled workers could earn more in America than in troubled homelands, sparked the **emigration** of an estimated **ten million Europeans** and **Asians** to the United States during the Gilded Age. Most of these immigrants came from the harsh climate of northern European countries. The railroads were the major employer, but opportunities were also abundant in factories, mining, farming, finance, and many other trades and occupations.

Upon completion of the railroad, many immigrant laborers who had worked on the western tracks looked to the mining industry for jobs, and hundreds came to prospect or seek employment in Park City. Prospectors usually set up camps around their claims. The posh midsection of Deer Valley Resort, now called **Silver Lake**, was once the location of the first mining camp, called Lake Flat.

Park City's early settlers proved to have a civic spirit They established a **free public school** in 1875 which provided instruction for both children and adults, including immigrants and the illiterate who had never had access to formal education.

In the latter part of the decade the **Ontario Mine** became one of the leading silver producers in the world.

1880s: Early in this decade, railroad spur lines were completed from Coalville to both Kimball Junction and Park City. To keep building tracks, **trees were felled at great rates** and some skilled lumberjacks, called "tie hacks", could fabricate railroad ties right where the trees were chopped down. **Coal** from the mines of Coalville **powered the railroad** steam engines, providing the high capacity transport needed to make large-scale mining profitable. The days of using horses to pull wagons full of heavy rocks were ending, though horses would haul logs out of the forest until they started to be replaced by gasoline engines in the 1920s.

Expansion of the railroads enabled transport of bigger and better equipment to improve mine productivity. Mines such as the Mayflower, Woodside, Crescent, and numerous others arose to compete with the Ontario. Mine expansion fueled town growth, and Park City was legally incorporated in 1884.

Railroad expansion also brought more laborers to Park City, and **mine expansion** lured destitute workers away from depleted mines in Scotland, Ireland, Scandinavia, and other locales. Cornish miners from the southern tip of England (Cornwall) were especially valued for their hard rock engineering skills. Also present were many Chinese laborers. Due to hardship in China and economic opportunity promised by the California Gold Rush, and then by construction of the railroads, many Chinese men had migrated to California and the western United States during the previous two decades. Even little old Park City had a Chinatown, located where the China Bridge parking structure now stands on the east side of "Swede" Alley.

Chinese immigrants were appreciated for being especially skilled and eager workers. They were particularly adept at dangerous jobs involving explosives, essential to railroad construction, but their willingness to work for lower wages, along with the foreignness of their language and customs, generated wide spread resentment of these immigrants. Chinese job seekers were not hired as miners in Park City, but became cooks and launderers and filled positions that others wouldn't. The so-called **China Bridge** was built in Park City so that Caucasians could walk over instead of through the neighborhood where the Chinese resided. Ultimately Chinese workers were blamed for unemployment in other populations, prompting the federal government under President Chester A. Arthur (1881-85) to pass the Chinese Exclusion Act of 1882, greatly restricting Chinese immigration to the United States. In 1886, the *Park Record* newspaper proclaimed the "Chinese Must Go". (The Chinese Exclusion Act was repealed in 1943 when China became an American ally against Imperial Japan, but Chinese immigration to the USA remained severely restricted until the Immigration Act of 1965.)

Also in the 1880's **engineering technology** in the mining industry reached new heights and depths. A supersized Cornish Pump was transported from Philadelphia to Park City by freight train to remove water from constantly flooded mine tunnels. This device could extract four million gallons (15 million L) of water a day from a thousand feet below ground. However, as the mining tunnels reached lower levels, engineers such as **John Keetley** developed enormous drainage tunnels under the mountains to get rid of the water. It took laborers about six years of working day and night to build the 5-mile (8 km) long Keetley Drain Tunnel, 1,500 feet (457+ m) below ground, and its two ends met exactly in the middle as planned. Today, the Keetley and Spiro Drain Tunnels provide portions of Park City's municipal water supply.

By the mid-1880s the need for lumber for both fuel and construction·had ravaged forests on Park City's mountainsides. Then, without trees to stop snow and wet soil from cascading down steep inclines, winter **avalanches** and spring **mudslides** started to destroy mining camps. One heavy snow year, 84 people died in avalanches in Ontario Canyon, prompting miners to move down into the growing town.

In 1889 flourishing Park City became one of the first localities in Utah to have **electric light**. Candles, oil lamps, and the many fires they started were on the wane.

1890s: A **rail line between Park City** and **Salt Lake City** was completed, facilitating travel and transport of ore to a Salt Lake City smelter. The process of smelting (roasting) rocks to remove precious metals dates back about 2,700 years, when humans first learned how to get the lead out.

In spite of economic downturn during this decade, Park City mines continued to be productive and the **Silver King Mine** became another industry giant. Its mill still stands near the Bonanza chairlift at the Park City Resort. Mills separate rocks containing precious metals from useless rock, reducing the cost of transporting heavy ore to a smelter.

In 1898 a **Great Fire** of uncertain cause incinerated about 200 Park City businesses and residences, leaving some 500 people homeless. Chinatown was obliterated and never recovered, but profits from the mines, charitable contributions, and the determination of the citizens resulted in prompt reconstruction. As you walk through Old Town today, notice that many buildings show architectural features that were fashionable at the turn of the 19th century.

1900s: This decade gave birth to aviation, the Model-T automobile, the New York City subway system, Freudian psychology, silent movies, and the first baseball World Series. In 1901, Theodore (Teddy) Roosevelt (TR) became the youngest man to ascend to the presidency upon the assassination of President William McKinley. Through 1909, TR propelled the United States into a **Progressive Era** by pursuing regulation of the railroads, foods and drugs, by breaking up big trusts, and by promising fairness for all citizens. Originally from New York City, TR had worked as a rancher in the Dakotas and authored several nature books. As president, he made conservation of natural resources a priority, establishing some of the first **national parks, forests** and **monuments,** of which Utah has an especially generous share.

Park City's mines continued to profit in the 1900s but also experienced tragedy when an **explosion** in the Daly West Mine **killed 34 miners** in 1902, just as the city was recovering from the Great Fire. The 30-mile trip to a Salt Lake City hospital had been a hardship for injured miners, especially in winter. Soon after the catastrophe, social and fraternal organizations, private citizens, and the local miners' labor union came together to fund and build the **Miners Hospital** in 1904.

Legends about the ghosts of deceased miners are often heard in old mining towns. In Park City such ghosts came to be called **"Tommy Knockers"**. If you do hear thuds in the earth while walking about Park City, it is most likely due to settling of the ground within the hundreds of miles of tunnels that the miners blasted through these mountains.

19-Teens: The main event of this decade was World War One (1914-1918), along with the opening of the Panama Canal. The Emperor of China was forced to abdicate after 2,000 years of Imperial Rule, and the Russian Revolution overthrew 300 years of rule by the Romanov Dynasty. Stainless steel was invented and Ford motor company introduced the assembly line. In New York City, 25,000 women marched up Fifth Avenue to demand the right to vote.

Back in Park City during this decade, a Madam **Rachel Urban**, along with her husband George, was operating 16 houses of prostitution, called "cribs", on what are now Heber Avenue and Deer Valley Drive. One building featured a bar and piano player, while the rest of the cribs were single rooms. The neighborhood was called "The Row", "The Line", and the "Red Light District". The latter term may exist because railroad workers' carried red lanterns at night, which they left outside crib doors to show they were in use.

Single women were scarce in Park City's early days and for many single miners, cribs, saloons, and occasional community dances were the only available places to enjoy female companionship. In the 1800s, miners had been required by federal law to live in boarding houses provided by the mine operators. Even after this law was repealed in 1901, for many of these young men, boarding houses with strict rules were still the only available housing.

Rachel Urban has been described as a physically enormous woman with a wooden leg. It's said that she birthed six children, only one of whom survived, and kept a cussing parrot on her parlor porch. She came to be called Mother Urban because she took excellent care of her employees, who in turn took good care of the town's laborers and millionaires. She had a physician provide regular check-ups for her workers, threw Christmas parties for single miners, and helped the illiterate to write letters home. She paid substantial fines and taxes for her property and business and was a welcome contributor to the city's coffers. It's also said that she provided financial assistance to Park City's needy, coming to their doors after dark to protect their privacy. Rachel Urban died in 1933, and a popular jazz club called Mother Urban's Rathskeller, operated on Heber Avenue until 2005.

Another successful Park City Madam was **Bessie Wheeler**. She reportedly took in derelicts to rehabilitate them, cared for sick miners, and sent Christmas money to needy families. Stories about these Madams leaves one to wonder if entrepreneurial, philanthropic women of this era had so few opportunities, that **prostitution** was about the only accessible profession through which they could earn enough money to fulfill their missions of helping others. Certainly for some uneducated, orphaned girls and runaways, prostitution was a means of survival.

Although prostitution was a thriving quasi-legal industry in Park City from the 1870s through the 1950s, it wasn't always legal to operate a saloon. A **temperance movement** had been growing around the country since the 1840s, especially in the western United States where there was much religious piety. Utah was one of 33 states to ban the manufacture and distribution of alcohol (1917), even before the United States Congress did the same with the National Prohibition (Volstead) Act of 1919, and the 18th amendment to the U.S. Constitution in 1920.

Illegal stills came into existence as soon as **prohibition** did, especially in big cities and western mining towns. Miners had few remedies to relieve the pain of their physical toil. Their average lifespan wasn't much more than 40 years. Their pay was a few dollars a day and they had no health benefits, just enormous health risks. **Smoking opium** was another way some relieved pain, until the Harrison Act outlawed opium in 1914. (Prohibition of alcohol was a dismal failure that spawned rampant crime, and in 1933, the 21st amendment to the constitution repealed the 18th amendment, giving control of alcohol back to the states.)

1920s: Some notable events of this decade include **women** gaining the right to **vote** in 1920, and the first Olympic **Winter Games** in Chamonix, France in 1924. The Indian Citizenship Act of 1924 finally granted Native Americans U.S. citizenship. The discovery of penicillin in 1928 ushered in the age of modern medicine.

Park City and its mining industry continued to prosper throughout the 1920s until the Stock Market crashed in 1929, starting the **Great Depression**. In spite of prohibition, about two-dozen rollicking Park City saloons continued to illegally serve bootlegged alcoholic beverages during the "roaring 20s".

1930s: The Great Depression started in the United States but quickly lead to **worldwide financial collapse.** International trade plummeted 50% and there were big drops in the price of lead and silver, wounding Park City's economy. President Franklin Roosevelt was elected in 1932 and initiated the New Deal to combat widespread unemployment and poverty. The Works Progress Administration (WPA) was a program that paid the unemployed to build needed public works such as schools and bridges in almost every community. In Park City, the WPA built boarding houses and the **first ski trails** for a winter carnival in 1936. (The WPA ended in 1943 when war created a shortage of workers.)

In 1932, the Great Lake Timber Company held the title of Park City's second largest employer after the mines. The timber company was called the **"pole plant"** because it provided utility poles to proliferating electric and telephone companies all over the west, until it literally **ran out of timber**.

Alta Ski Area, a few miles south of Park City, opened its first ski lift in 1939, as war was breaking out in Europe.

1940s: The United States entered World War Two (1939-1945) after the Japanese bombed Pearl Harbor in 1941. President Roosevelt died in office, never seeing the war's end that followed the U.S. nuclear attack of Hiroshima, Japan on August 6, 1945.

The war helped to bring about the recovery of the American economy, and in 1946, a T-bar ski lift was built out of some of the last surviving lodge-pole pine trees, creating the **Snow Park Ski Area** on slopes that would ultimately become Deer Valley Resort. Lift tickets cost one dollar. However, the price of silver and lead spiraled downwards after the war, and in the summer of 1949, more than a thousand miners were thrust out of work when the Park City **mines abruptly closed**.

1950s: Post war America was a time of economic growth and the rise of the middle class and suburbia, but not for Park City. Although some of the mines re-opened, residents were moving away and businesses were closing. Tourism further declined after authorities shut down the red light district in 1955. While the rest of America was enjoying a baby boom, television, rock and roll, racial desegregation, polio immunization, and the rise of Las Vegas as the new "sin city", Park City was being referred to as a "ghost town".

1960s: To revive the shattered economy, the last surviving mining company, **United Park City Mines**, procured a loan from the administration of President John F. Kennedy to open **Treasure Mountains Ski Area** in 1963. To attract skiers, the longest gondola in the U.S.A. was installed, along with a double chair lift and a J-bar. Olympic ski celebrity **Stein Erikson** was hired as ski school director to bolster the resort's glitterati appeal. Initially lift tickets cost $3.50. (The resort was renamed Park City Ski Area in 1966 and when snowboarding became popular, the name was changed to Park City Mountain Resort in 1996.)

Mining history is commemorated by the names of many of the resort's ski runs. There are lifts and trails called Silver King, Silver Queen, Silver Star, Silver Skis, Silver Lode and Silver Hollow. Other mining associated names are: Prospector, Lost Prospector, Treasure Hollow, Glory Hole, Mother Lode, Bonanza, and Claim Jumper. Some other trail names related to mining are: Shaft, Hoist, Dynamite, Powder Keg, Nail Driver, and Widow Maker. The "widow-maker" was a miner's drill that created enough silica dust to cause premature death from lung failure.

Ski slopes with names like Single Jack, Double Jack, Muckers, and Powder Monkey honor some of the miners' jobs. Before the pneumatic drill, miners blasted through rock by one man swinging a 4-pound (1.8 kg) hammer against a drill bit, referred to as "Single-Jacking." "Double Jacking" describes two men doing this job, one swinging an 8-pound (3.6 kg) hammer and the other holding the drill bit against the rock. It took about 50 hammer strikes to be effective. The "Powder Monkey" was the miner who handled the explosives. After a successful blast, a "Mucker" came along with a shovel to load the broken rock into a mine car. As you might imagine, any "Tommy Knockers" haunting the resorts nowadays are much more likely to be "powder monkey" miners than powder skiers.

Also amongst the mining relics at Park City Resort is the Silver King Boarding House, built in 1896. With electricity and hot and cold running water, it was a marvel for its time. It once provided meals to a thousand miners a day. In 1987 it was pushed up the mountain by bulldozers and renovated to become a slope-side restaurant.

In 1968 **Park West Ski Area** opened just north of Park City Resort. Its name has since been changed to Wolf Mountain, then The Canyons, and currently, the Canyons Village at Park City Resort.

1970s: Major events of this decade included the end of the war in Viet Nam, the beginning of the computer age, a gas shortage creating "oily" world politics, and the Watergate scandal and 1974 resignation of President Richard M. Nixon. Back in Park City in 1974, a woman became a miner for the first time in the town's history just as the mines were gasping their last breath. It took more than 100 years and the women's liberation movement to squelch the superstition that females brought bad luck to mines.

1980s: This decade saw a **nuclear disaster** in Chernobyl, the collapse of Soviet communism, and the birth of Microsoft Windows and magnetic resonance imaging (MRI).

Skiing succeeded in bringing residents and tourists back to Park City and in 1981, **Deer Valley Ski Area** was created with five lifts on Bald and Bald Eagle Mountains.

Also in 1981 The Utah/US Film Festival moved from Salt Lake City to Park City, and later came under the direction of Robert Redford as the **Sundance Film Festival.** Park City's recovery was also marked by the birth of its own radio station, KPCW, in 1980, and its own television station, TV45, in 1986.

1990s: The creation of the **Internet** in 1991 and Operation Desert Storm in Iraq and Kuwait both changed the world. For Park City, the turn of the millennium was marked by residential expansion and the town's recognition as a winter sports mecca. Park City Mountain, Deer Valley, and The Canyons Resorts were frequently rated in the favorites lists of winter sports publications.

2000s-Present: The successful 2002 Salt Lake City **Olympic Winter Games,** staged six months after the **9/11** terrorist attacks, brought Park City international fame. The Deer Valley and Park City Resorts hosted most of the ski and snowboard events. The Utah Olympic Park in Kimball Junction provided venues for bobsled, luge, skeleton, and ski jumping. You can still watch athletes training at these facilities and in the ski resort terrain parks and half-pipes.

In 2008 *Forbes Traveler Magazine* named Park City one of the 20 **prettiest towns** in America.

Park City was designated a **Gold-Level Ride Center** by the International Mountain Bicycling Association in 2011, the first global biking destination to be so rated. Also in 2011, *The New York Times* ranked Park City as #9 of the 40 **top resort** places to go.

In 2013 Park City received Google's **eCity Award** for the strongest online business community in the state, and *Outside Magazine* selected Park City as the winner of the **Best Active Town in America** Award.

In 2014 Vail Resorts purchased Park City Mountain Resort and in 2015, built a gondola to connect it with The Canyons Resort to create the **largest ski area** in the United States. Vail's presence in Park City augments the town's international stardom as Vail sells its Epic ski passes globally, especially in the southern hemisphere where vacationers like to escape summer heat and spend a white Christmas in a ski town.

In 2015 *Fodor's Travel* identified 25 global can't-miss places to visit, rating the state of **Utah** as **"The Top Destination"** of the year. Also in 2015, Park City was designated the **"friendliest place in America"** by *Conde Nast Traveler* magazine.

As you walk around Park City today, it may be difficult to visualize the tiny, primitive, polluted mining town that popped up here in the wilderness a century and a half ago, but the walks in this book will acquaint you with many of the landmarks that can connect you with the town and its people's colorful past history.

~The Ecology Of Park City~

Walkers will encounter an amazing assortment of wildlife, vegetation, geologic phenomena, and microclimates in their travels around Park City. **Ecology** is the study of the relationships of life forms to one another and to the elements of their environment.

ANIMALS

Birds are the animals most likely seen on Park City walks, along with human accompanied dogs. Also common are chipmunks, squirrels, porcupines, marmots, foxes, raccoons, and little prairie dog-like critters called "potguts". The night hunter skunk is more often smelled than seen.

Utah "potguts" are ground squirrels that hibernate about 9 months a year. Photo by Pixabay.com

    Moose, elk and **deer** reside all around Park City, occasionally stroll through neighborhoods, and are too often encountered crossing roads when the first snow prompts their migration to winter ranges. Coyotes, cougars (a.k.a. mountain lions), bobcats and bear are rarely seen. Muskrats and trout in ponds and streams are frequently observed.

Warning: Highly intelligent magpies like to steal lunches and jewelry. Photo by Pixabay.com

    Birds most likely noticed include magpies, robins, swallows, mourning doves and sparrows. Hummingbirds, chickadees, cowbirds, woodpeckers, finches, and killdeers are also common. Eagles, owls, osprey, and falcons rule the skies, and a variety of hawks will challenge identification skills. Quail (mountain chickens) occasionally startle winter walkers by popping out of snow banks. Sandhill cranes can stand four feet (122 cm) tall and make trumpeting calls that can shake you out of bed.

    Canada geese and mallard ducks are regular residents, while other varieties of waterfowl stop over during migrations. Bluebird houses have been built along some trails to attract these beauties. Also common are crows, ravens, grackles, flickers, kestrels, grosbeaks, red-winged blackbirds, and others too numerous to mention.

    Critters you are unlikely to encounter in Park City include biting insects and poisonous snakes that prefer lower altitudes. However, traditional wildlife ranges may be altered by climate change, so there are no guarantees. **Diamondback rattlesnakes** reside at elevations

Sandhill crane couples return to their same nesting grounds every spring. Photo by J.F. Klimasiewfski

just a few hundred feet (a hundred or so meters) lower than Park City. Heavy rains can bring mosquitoes. It's likely that wildlife encounters will increase as people build deeper and deeper into the animals' habitat.

VEGETATION

Park City's native plants vary widely from place to place, depending on the day, which way the compass points, and at what elevation you are walking. Park City's climate can be dually classified. Geographically, the town is located on the Colorado plateau, characterized by a high desert climate, but its mountains represent a temperate co-niferous forest. In other words, there is just enough precipitation in the form of snow at higher elevations to support the tall trees that grow on Park City's mountainsides.

At elevations starting around 6,000 feet (1,829 m), the setting of most of these walks, the **pine-oak zone** of trees predominates. Above 8,000 feet (2,438 m), the fir-aspen zone prevails. Visually, tall trees thrive on the mountainous west and south sides of Park City, while small trees survive to the north and east. Most of the scrubby little trees one sees there are gambel oak, which grow in thickets, providing shelter and food for deer. Orange lichens growing on the bark are harmless. Also common in the pine-oak zone is drought-tolerant mountain mahogany, while chokecherry and cottonwood trees prefer the moisture of stream banks.

In the **fir-aspen zone**, Douglas fir, subalpine fir, and Engelmann spruce trees dominate north-facing slopes. Aspens rule on south-facing terrain.

Prickly pear cactuses all look the same until each blooms a uniquely colored flower.

A great variety of **wildflowers** can be found around Park City, with different species thriving in different zones. Blooming seasons also vary from year to year, depending on temperatures and precipitation levels. To catch the single week of summer that the prickly pears bloom along the west facing Lah Dee Duh Trail, I might have to walk there every week of June, or pos-sibly miss this flower show.

Penstemon and paintbrushes (prairie fire) provide a perfusion of blues and reds on north facing slopes. There are about 200 species of paintbrush in the west-ern United States. Their flowers are edible but other parts of the plant are toxic.

Paintbrushes bloom along many Park City trails from spring through fall.
Photo by Ken Hurwitz MD

Wild pink roses and multicolored columbine are common at higher altitudes. Wild geraniums and lupines border low-lying trails. Numerous sun-flower species splash landscapes with yellow, and wild onions with lavender flowers are prolific in spring. The variety of wild flowers that bloom at different times and altitudes always amazes.

Berries also thrive in Park City's mountains. Wild black currants, elderberries, serviceberries, gooseberries, raspberries, and snowberries, are a few of the fruits that support local wildlife.

MINERALS

Park City is a living laboratory for **geology**, the study of Earth and its history by analysis of its rocks and minerals, and land and water formations. Park City's terrain was shaped by millions of years of geological processes including the deposition of natural materials by ancient oceans, uplift of the mountains and sinking of the Salt Lake Valley along the **Wasatch Fault**, transport and fracture of rocks by glaciers and rivers, and continuous erosion by snow, rain and wind. **Precious metals** in Park City's rugged terrain gave birth to the town. Typically, it took one ton (907 kg) of ore to produce one pound (0.45 kg) of silver. From that same ton of ore, called **galena**, miners also recovered lead and zinc, but hundreds of pounds (kgs) of each ton of rock were useless ("mine tailings" or "gangue") and were left in piles around the mountains.

The largest piece of galena on record was 10 inches (25cm) in length, width and height. Photo by Pixabay.com

Local terrain also provides building materials such as sandstone and you'll encounter some **quarries** on some of these walks. Regional bedrock consists of Jurassic quartzite, limestone, sandstone, siltstone, mudstone, shale, and intrusive rocks added by glaciers and volcanoes.

Melting snow unearths geologic history every spring. A walker might notice shells, marine fossils, stone artifacts like arrowheads, bits of galena, or perhaps, pieces of volcanic lava or meteorites. If walkers can shift their eyes from the magnificent macro-views, a small treasure might be seen, but should be left in place for the next observant eye.

WEATHER

Weather phenomena in Park City can include any of these conditions, at least some of which are likable:

High heat in the late afternoon of long summer days is not a good time to walk along rocky ridges or on black pavement, especially with dogs and children who are low to the ground. Mid-summer's hottest hours often occur between five and seven in the evening. However, even the rare very hot days usually start with deliciously cool mornings.

Sunburn can occur even on cloudy days, especially if there's snow. Sunscreen and UV blocking sunglasses are always a must and should be worn on cloudy as well as bright days. **Ultraviolet light is more intense at altitude**. UV blockage by sunglasses is independent of lens color, but yellow lenses enhance vision in low light.

Rapid temperature drops in the evening should be expected, even in mid-summer. Take an extra layer if you plan to walk as the sun drops behind the mountains.

A **sundog** is a rainbow halo around the sun and/or bright spots on each side of the sun. Also called a parhelion, this phenomenon is created by the bending of light by ice crystals in high clouds.

A sundog may indicate impending stormy weather. Photo by Basu Ghosh

Lightning, sudden **downpours** and monster **hail** can occur any time of year, but are most likely in hot weather. Bring a wide brimmed, waterproof hat or thin plastic poncho with you on days with possibility of thunderstorms. In the presence of lightning, **get away from rocky ridges, open fields** and **lone trees.** You're safer crouching down in a cluster of tall brush or small trees.

Rapid weather changes are entirely normal. Locals say: "if you don't like the weather, wait five minutes".

Note the colors of the double rainbows are not identical, but mirror images. Photo by Pixabay.com

Double rainbows often follow summer rain. Rainbows might be seen whenever there are drops of water in the air and the sun is shining from a low point in the sky behind the observer. Even a water fountain or garden hose can create a rainbow if the sun angle is right. A second rainbow may appear when light is reflected from within the raindrops as well as off of the raindrop backs.

Virga is rain that evaporates before touching the ground, as observed from a distance. You may be walking in sunshine while watching cloudbursts all around you.

Inversions (of temperature) occur in winter. Park City can be ten or more degrees F (6-7° C) cooler than Salt Lake City in the summer, but just as many degrees warmer in winter. When cold fog hangs over the valleys, persons who ascend the mountains can find clear sunny skies and the higher you go, the warmer it gets.

Snow squalls are micro-storms of swirling snow that last a few minutes, usually in winter, but they can occur almost any time of year at higher elevations. Blizzards are infrequent in Utah, much to the chagrin of skiers. Park City's snow has tended to fall in dribs and drabs in recent years, as weather systems move rapidly through the mountains.

Avalanches may occur whenever there's snow in the mountains. Local news sources provide avalanche risk reports daily in winter. You may also wake up to "dynamite reveille," early on snowy mornings. That's the sound of explosions set off in unstable snow to trigger avalanches before skiers arrive at the resorts. Find up-to-date information about avalanche risks at utahavalanchecenter.org.

Arctic Clippers are blasts of very cold air, occurring occasionally in December or January and increasing risk of **frostbite.** Typically, Utah winters are not bitter cold and a 32 degree F (0 degree C) day can feel warm when the sun is high.

Windstorms are most likely to occur in spring. Pockets of high winds can also be encountered along ridgelines and at the mouths of canyons. Since having the wind at your back when walking uphill may be preferred, you might want to reverse the direction of the walks in this guide, depending on which way the wind blows. Prevailing winds come from the west. Some localities in Park City also get swirling winds. If walking on wooded trails on a very windy day, be aware of the possibility of falling trees, especially if the trees appear unhealthy. Aspens throughout the western United States are suffering from blight.

Seismic tremors occur occasionally, and **landslides** and **rockslides** are rare but possible.

Fire is the number one threat to most communities in the western United States. While lightning and drought-stricken trees are primary risk factors, many forests and homes are lost because of thoughtless people who toss cigarettes, light firecrackers, fail to extinguish campfires, or go target shooting on windy days. Wind can also carry smoke from very remote fires to Park City's blue skies.

Finally, spectacular **sunrises** and **sunsets** occur almost daily.

Notice: Weather and avalanche conditions are predicted and reported by local news and Internet sources daily. However, walkers must appreciate that the **timing and localization of mountain weather is notoriously unpredictable**.

~Before You Go: Etiquette and Safety~

There are some rules, laws, and common sense expectations that local walkers should be familiar and compliant with to stay safe and optimize the walking experience:

Don't tackle physical activity at **high altitude** that you are unaccustomed to. If you are new to high altitude, especially if arriving from sea level, be especially cautious. Even very fit persons can be genetically susceptible to high altitude sickness. Make sure you feel comfortable at 7,000 feet (2,134 m) before undertaking demanding exercise.

Headache, nausea, fatigue, insomnia, and shortness of breath are common symptoms of **altitude intolerance**. Drinking more water and going to a lower altitude are therapeutic. Some altitude-sensitive persons will do best sleeping at a lower altitude and gradually increasing daytime exposure to higher elevations. For others, dinner in Heber City at an elevation of c.5,600 feet (1,707 m), or Salt Lake City, at c.4,200 feet (1,280 m), may be just what the doctor orders.

Back in Park City, **smile** at passersby. This town is full of fascinating people and potentially great encounters. In neighborhoods unaccustomed to walkers, a friendly demeanor can allay suspicions.

Be prepared to **share** roads and trails with motorists, dog walkers, cyclists, skaters, equestrians, snow-shoers, skiers, etc., and be warned: they haven't all read the rules. Cyclists and skiers can go very fast without making a sound, or wind might blow warnings out of earshot. Some are inexperienced and can't stop, even though the walker has the right of way. When on busy paths or trails, **use your ears for safety** instead of music or conversation. **Warn others when passing**.

When on roads traveled by motorized vehicles, pedestrians should **walk towards oncoming traffic** on the left side of the road. On paved trails that prohibit motorized vehicles, pedestrians usually walk on the right side. However, in areas of heavy traffic, it may occasionally be safer to walk on the left and get off of the path if cyclists or skiers coming from opposite directions have to pass each other.

When allowing cyclists to pass on narrow single-track on hills, **step to the higher side** of the trail if possible, to reduce the risk of getting knocked downhill.

When on busy trails or roadsides with narrow shoulders, **walk single file**. Also, consider that walking in large groups may be unsettling to neighborhoods or wildlife. A youth group leader might want to divide walkers into pairs and trios.

Road crossings are minimal for most of these walks. Use crosswalks with pedestrian controlled pushbuttons when available. Realize there are many tourists in Park City who may be unfamiliar with the roads, roundabouts, winter driving conditions, their rental vehicle, etc. Even at quiet crosswalks, exercise caution. Try to **make eye contact with drivers before entering a crosswalk** to be sure they are attentive. If not on phones, some drivers are gawking at the gorgeous scenery or at spandex-clad cyclists; or they're gawking while on their phones.

Be visible. An early sign of cataracts is when an unaware driver can't distinguish between the side of the road and a walker in gray pants and a green shirt. If you walk at dawn or dusk, wear reflective tape front and back. I attach a blinking light to my dog's collar.

Respect fences, barricades and '**No Trespassing**" signs. All of the land around Park City is private property. Ownership can change or a neighborhood could become gated. If you mistakenly wind up on private land and are confronted by a displeased owner, respectfully apologize and ask for instructions back to a public trail.

Respect the land. Forging a path up a steep slope as a shortcut to walking switchbacks may be quicker for you, but it causes erosion. When off-road, stay on trails.

Stay off muddy trails. In spring or after heavy rain, muddy trails can instantly become rutty. Tracks in mud can ruin a trail for the entire season and lead to erosion. If you encounter a muddy trail, turn around and find another place to walk. If you come upon muddy sections of trail, it is kinder to the trail to walk through the middle of the puddles than to carve trails around the puddles.

Equestrians are infrequently encountered around Park City, but all other trail users are obliged to yield to them. **Horses spook easily.** Do your best not to startle them.

No animal likes being snuck up on. **Make some noise** from a distance if you see a wild animal before she sees you, especially in spring when she might be protecting babies, or in mating season in the fall.

Do not approach or **feed wild animals**. Wild animals that are unafraid of people may be sick or rabid. Their friendliness can put you or them in danger.

Be extra **alert at dawn** and **dusk** when animals are more active. Walking in small groups is a good idea at these times, as is keeping your ears open to hear animal noise. Don't allow small children or dogs to appear separated from the adults.

Never approach a carcass. Predators may be guarding their kill. There are signs posted at some of the trailheads in this book that advise specific behaviors for the possibility of encountering a potentially dangerous wild animal. Read and heed these signs.

All **dogs are required to be on leashes** in all public places including trails, with the exception of designated off-leash trails and dog-parks. Park City used to be such a dog-friendly place; it was affectionately called "Bark City". Unfortunately, irresponsible dog owners have ruined dog freedom for all. There are **leash police** in Park City who ticket and fine owners of free running dogs. If pooches aren't going to be altogether banned, dog walkers should always take responsibility for their pets' behavior and waste, even on dirt trails. Some trailheads provide pick-up bags (mutt-mitts), but please bring your own in case these are not available.

Of all the walks in this book, I know of only a few short sections of trail that disallow leashed dogs in some residential areas of the Deer Valley Duck Ponds, Walk #6. Some other walks are noted as not ideal for dogs. There are **off-leash dog-parks** available at Walks #22, #23 and #29. Find **off-leash dog trails** in Trailside Park and on the Run-A-Muk Trail, on the south side of Olympic Parkway. In 2016, some Round Valley trails and the Old Town library field were opened to off-leash dogs under voice control, on a trial basis.

If you walk an **unfriendly dog**, please put a **yellow ribbon** or bandana on the leash or collar to warn others. The "yellow dog" project aims to help the nervous dog as well as dog lovers who might otherwise approach a pet that would be better off left alone.

Personally, I've never encountered a dog that was unwilling to share the trail on thousands of miles of Park City walks. Wish I could say the same about people. I often carry a metal thermos with a strong strap that would give a cruel bop to the snout of an aggressive animal if I could manage to swing it; but fortunately, I've never needed to try that. More often, walking with dogs leads to great encounters with friendly people.

It is **legal** for a shepherd, rancher or ranger **to kill a dog** that is harassing sheep, cattle, other livestock, or wildlife. Shepherds occasionally move flocks through local terrain. Goats have been employed for summer weed control at the resorts. What dog wouldn't love to chase a goat? Please protect your self, pets, and others by leashing the dog.

Do not drink water from natural sources. Mountain streams may contain high levels of heavy metals, bacteria or other contaminants. There are streams along some of these walks that dogs like to drink from, but I would rather my dogs did not drink this water and I always carry water for them.

Please **share nature's gifts.** Leave flowers unpicked and the pretty rock unturned for the next observer to enjoy. It's always sad to see a wilted bouquet thrown to the ground at the end of someone's walk. Even plunged into a water bottle, fragile wildflowers will likely not survive beyond the ride home.

Leave nothing behind. There are recycle containers, dog waste stations, and/or other waste receptacles at some trailheads and at most community facilities. If there isn't, take trash with you and dispose of it properly.

Winter walkers will be delighted to know that snow gets packed down on many miles of local trails. Go to www.parkcity.org/departments/trails/winter-trails for information about winter trail grooming and conditions.

On roads and sidewalks, winter walking conditions can be very variable with areas of dry pavement interspersed with **"black ice"** in shady spots. Black ice occurs when ice contains so little water that it doesn't glisten and you can't see it. Appropriate footwear is critical to your safety, but even if you are very sure-footed and have excellent tread on your shoes, you're no match for a skidding automobile on an icy hill. Be especially wary of icy conditions when the sun abruptly drops behind the mountains on warm winter afternoons. Another risk is **high snow banks** that prohibit drivers exiting driveways or turning a corner from seeing pedestrians.

There are still **mining relics** dotting Park City's landscapes, including old buildings, aerial tram towers, and mine shafts all over the mountains. While effort has been made to reduce danger, walkers still need to exercise caution. Loose rocks traveling with spring run-off can expose mineshafts buried under rotted timbers. After heavy rain in May 2015, a structure from the Daly West Mine collapsed, leaving an open shaft 40 feet (12 m) across and 2,000 feet (610 m) deep. While city officials struggle with the preservation of these antiquities, walkers should keep a safe distance from roped off places.

Along with the rest of the Rocky Mountains, Park City's native aspen and cottonwood trees are in decline. **Avoid walking in woods** on the occasional **very windy day,** when some of the more diseased trees can come crashing down. Sometimes, when deep in the woods, you don't feel the wind; but creaking, cracking sounds are signs of tree distress.

Park City is really a very safe place to walk, if you discount slipping on ice while wearing inappropriate shoes. However, as a sometimes-lone walker, I am compelled to advise others: **avoid walking alone** in remote areas that you are not familiar with. If you walk alone, inform someone of where you are going and when you expect to be back, or leave behind information. Always carry with you the name and number of **who to contact** in case of emergency.

Pepper spray, as a means of self-defense, may require relatively close proximity to a dangerous being. Still, it is recommended for walkers in bear territory. A police whistle might be helpful in some situations. Personally, my only safety concern for local walks is speeding cyclists who don't give timely warnings. Hopefully this issue won't be aggravated by city hall's decision to allow electric bikes on some trails. Electric bikes should be applauded for boosting interest in cycling and allowing people with limited fitness to enjoy Park City's hilly terrain; but some such cyclists may not have the skill to navigate crowded trails, necessitating increased caution on the part of walkers. Staying alert and attuned to the environment and **anticipating the foibles of others** is the best self-defense.

Finally, safety is always dependent on being prepared for **weather changes**, as described in the previous chapter.

WALKING COMBOS OR NOT?

Listening to music or books on tape or talking on the phone might be okay if you're familiar with your route, there's no traffic, and you remain attentive to your surrounds and **leave one ear open**. However, an exciting story or engaging conversation could compromise your awareness or prevent you from hearing warnings from others.

Reading or texting while walking is never a good idea, although a local college has designated a campus lane for that dual purpose. If you must text along the way, stop walking and step out of harm's way.

Whistling, singing, or playing the harmonica or tambourine might be okay; if you are not disturbing neighbors or wildlife and you can still hear bike bells and voices.

Walkers can bird watch, people watch, business watch, construction watch, neighborhood watch and/or community watch. **Watching** can be more absorbing than walking.

Walkers can window shop and entrepreneurs can be their own walking billboards.

Walking can provide sustenance to photographers, artists, writers, poets, and composers. There is emerging evidence that workers are more creative and productive when walking is incorporated into their work schedule. At the headquarters of linkedin.com, meetings are reportedly held while walking. My training as a physician taught me that **learning** is greatly enhanced when lessons are transferred from classrooms to walking around where the patients are.

Going for a walk can be an emergency **anger management tool** for those moments in life when one contemplates far worse behavior. However, if someone is too upset to pay attention to what they are doing, they shouldn't be out walking around.

Mall walking may facilitate sticking to a walking program in inclement weather. Some urban walkers feel safer in malls than neighborhoods. Malls can provide long corridors of smooth surface, controlled climate, and lots of other amenities.

All kinds of **exercises can be combined** with walking such as stretching and rotation exercises of the neck, torso, shoulders, arms, and hands. Breathing or facial exercises can also be incorporated. Pockets can accommodate stretch bands or squeeze putty to work the upper extremities, though serious walkers believe that arms should swing freely and would not carry anything by hand, especially not weights.

Meditating, praying or engaging in mental exercise could be distractions or enhancements of the walking experience, depending on how you do it.

The use of walking poles or snowshoes can add terrain and seasons to one's routine, as well as improve stamina, strength and aerobic capacity; but there are other resources for that. This book is about basic walking.

Can you **chew gum** and **walk** at the same time? Fatal asphyxiation due to aspiration of candy or chewing gum while walking, is not as rare as it should be.

Warning: Distracted walking is more dangerous than distracted driving. **In collisions, pedestrians are almost always the losers.**

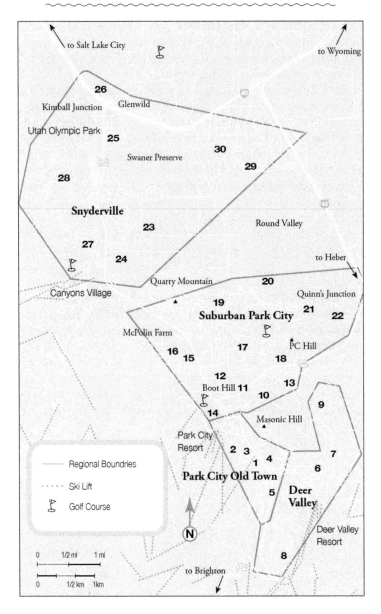

Overview Map: The walks in this book are divided into 4 regions.
This map shows the regions and the approximate location of each walk.

ABOUT THE INFORMATION IN THIS BOOK

All but a few of these walks are readily accessible by Park City's free bus transportation. **Bus** schedules and routes vary from season to season. **Information** is available at www.parkcity.org/about-us/transit-bus, by calling 435.615.5301, on signs at bus stops, and on brochures inside the buses. Buses are equipped to carry wheelchairs and a limited number of bicycles. Only certified service animals are allowed to accompany humans on the buses.

Although walks in this book are all accessible by bus or walking, **parking** information is available for all walks. Parking in an unauthorized place often results in towing, significant expense, and a big hassle. For some walks with limited parking, the bus is the best option.

Maps of the walks in this guide identify bus stops, parking areas, and other landmarks where applicable. **Distances** and **elevations** are **approximate.** They were computed using the smart phone app www.mapmywalk.com/. Fractions are rounded off. If you track these same walks using a GPS app, your readings may differ.

At the time this book and its maps were created the name "Park City Mountain Resort" was changed to "Park City Resort", but both names remain in use along with the name "Park City Mountain". It's all the same place.

All of the walks in this book are configured as loops. If you are interested in accessing connecting trails, retailers such as local bike shops sell the trail map produced annually by the Mountain Trails Foundation. At the website mountaintrails. org, you'll find interactive maps and up-to-date information about **trail conditions** or **closures** due to mud, maintenance or events like races. Please don't wander into off-road terrain without consulting appropriate resources to insure that you don't become an illegal intruder, lost, or carried off by a mudslide.

Restrooms are available for most of these walks as described, and for most of these walks, privacy is available only in restrooms.

Please be aware that frequent website changes may make some of the URL addresses referenced in this guidebook outdated.

Notice: Trails, paths, roads and landmarks noted for any of the routes in this book may change. New construction or new property ownership may **delete** or **reroute some of these walks**. Street signs and trail markers may not always be present and occasionally signs get twisted around to point the wrong way. Sometimes wildlife creates new **"fooler" trails** when nature provides them a new food source. Also realize that maps on GPS satellite systems, as well as maps in this book, may lag behind changes in roads, and trails. Please respect barricades and signs indicating Private Property or No Trespassing.

| | Walks By Region* with Degree of | | |
| | < Continued onto next page> | | |
Walk	Page #	Difficulty**
1. City Park-Main Street	32	I
2. Old Town Via PC Resort	36	D
3. Empire Ave-Park Ave	40	D
4. Masonic Hill-Deer Valley	44	I
5. Ontario Ridge-Rossi Hill	47	D
6. Deer Valley Duck Ponds	50	E
7. Deer Valley-Deer Crest	52	I
8. Silver Lake Village	55	E
9. Lower & Upper Deer Valley	57	I
10. Tour of Tunnels & Rail Trail	60	E
11. Olympic Plaza-Kearns Blvd	63	E
12. Boot Hill-McLeod Creek Trail	66	I
13. Chatham Hills-Prospector Square	69	I
14. Thaynes Canyon	71	I
15. Farm Trail-McLeod Creek Trail	74	I
16. Aspen Springs	78	I
17. Park Meadows	81	I
18. PC Hill	84	D
19. The Cove-Quarry Mountain	87	I
20. La Dee Duh	90	I
21. Fairway Hills	93	E
22. Quinn's Junction	96	E
23. Willow Creek Park	98	E
24. Matt Knoop Park-McLeod Creek	100	E
25. Swaner-Redstone	103	E
26. Over/Under Kimball Junction	105	E
27. The Canyons-Sun Peak	108	D
28. Bear Hollow-Olympic Park	111	D
29. Trailside Park	114	E
30. Mountain Ranch Estates	116	I

*Regions
Old Town 1-5
Deer Valley 6-9
Suburban Park City 10-22
Snyderville Basin 23-30

Difficulty**, Distance*** and Elevation Gain
< Continued from previous page>

Distance*** In Miles	Elevation Gain In Feet	Distance*** In Km	Elevation Gain In Meters
3.0	300	4.8	91
2.2	302	3.5	92
2.9	352	4.7	107
1.9	155	2.9	47
2.5	397	4.0	121
1-1.5	46	1.6-2.4	14
1.7	394	2.7	120
1.2	43	1.9	13
4.8	387	7.7	186
3.0	210	4.8	64
2.9	98	4.7	30
1.0	29	1.6	10
2.3	318	3.7	97
2.5	200	3.8	61
3.5	148	5.6	45
2.5	285	4.0	87
4.9	131	7.9	40
3.2	536	5.2	163
1.3	125	2.0	38
1.3	92	2.0	28
1.8	125	2.9	38
1.0	62	1.6	19
0. 3-1.8	70	0.5-2.9	21
2.5	161	4.0	49
1.5	33	2.4	10
2.8	148	4.5	45
3.0	272	4.8	83
6.7	892	10.8	272
0. 65-1.1	59-98	1.0-1.8	18-30
2.4	269	3.8	82

**** Degree of Difficulty**
E = Easy
I = Intermediate
D = Difficult
***Some of the shorter walks are easily combined with other walks as noted in directions.

Like the rating system for ski trails, **degree of difficulty** is relative only to the mountain you're on. The difficulty of these walks has been assessed with respect to distance, elevation gain, trail surface, and how each walk compares to the other included walks.

The Walks In Order of Estimated Degree of Difficulty			
Easy	**Easy to Intermediate**	**Intermediate to Difficult**	**Difficult**
23 Willow Creek Pk.	1 City Park-Main St.	7 DV*-Deer Crest	5 Ontario Ridge
22 Quinn's Junction.	14 Thaynes Canyon	13 Chatham Hills	2 Old Town
6 DV* Duck Ponds	30 Mt Ranch Estates	12 Boot Hill	18 PC Hill
8 Silver Lake	15 Farm-McLeod Cr.	17 Park Meadows	3 Empire-Park Ave.
29 Trailside Park	20 Lah Dee Duh	16 Aspen Springs	27 The Canyons
25 Swaner-Redstn	19 Cove-Quarry Mt.	9 Low & Up DV*	28 Olympic Park
21 Fairway Hills		4 Masonic Hill	
11 Oly Plaza-Kearns			
24 Matt Knoop Park			
26 Kimball Junction			
10 Tour of Tunnels	* DV = Deer Valley		

The easiest walks tend to have level surfaces and gentle inclines. Pavement is usually smooth enough for wheelchairs. Unpaved trails are without big rocks and roots. Some trails are groomed in winter making them accessible to short legs and ordinary winter shoes. www.parkcity.org/departments/open-space-and-trails provides winter trail information.

Walks of intermediate difficulty have inclines that are longer and/or steeper, but still manageable for moderately fit walkers. Some off-road walking is included.

For more difficult routes, walkers should be in good health and well conditioned. These walks involve long or steep inclines, longer distances, higher altitudes, or rougher terrain.

Time allotments for these walks are not specified. For the average leisure walker, 20-25 minutes per mile (1.6 km) is typical. Some people will need half or twice that amount of time.

Popular Walk Features	PAGE #	DINING	DOGS+	HISTORIC	KIDS^	OFF-ROAD*	SHOPPING	WHEELS^	WINTER++
1. City Park-Main Street	32	✔		✔	✔		✔	✔	✔
2. Old Town Via PC Resort	36	✔		✔	✔	✔	✔		
3. Empire Ave-Park Ave	40	✔		✔			✔		
4. Masonic Hill-Deer Valley	44			✔		✔			
5. Ontario Ridge-Rossi Hill	47			✔		✔			
6. Deer Valley Duck Ponds	50	✔	+			✔			
7. Deer Valley-Deer Crest	52	✔				*			
8. Silver Lake Village	55	✔					✔	✔	
9. Lower & Upper DV	57					*			
10. Tour of Tunnels & Rail Trl	60	✔		✔	✔		✔	✔	✔
11. Olympic Plaza-Kearns Blvd	63	✔		✔	✔	*	✔	✔	✔
12. Boot Hill-McLeod Crk Trl	66	✔				✔	✔		
13. Chatham Hills-Prospector	69	✔				*		*	✔
14. Thaynes Canyon	71	✔		✔		*		*	
15. Farm Trl-McLeod Crk Trl	74	✔	+	✔				✔	
16. Aspen Springs	78		+					*	✔
17. Park Meadows	81		+		✔			✔	✔
18. PC Hill	84		+			✔			
19. The Cove-Quarry Mt	87		+			✔			
20. La Dee Duh	90		+			✔			✔
21. Fairway Hills	93		+			✔			✔
22. Quinn's Junction	96		✔		✔	✔			✔
23. Willow Creek Park	98		✔		✔	*		✔	✔
24. Matt Knoop-McLeod Crk	100		+		✔	*		✔	✔
25. Swaner-Redstone	103	✔	+	✔			✔	✔	✔
26. Over/Under Kimball Jncn	105	✔			✔	*	✔	*	✔
27. The Canyons-Sun Peak	108	✔	+	✔				*	✔
28. Bear Hollow-Olympic Pk	111	✔		✔	✔		✔	*	✔
29. Trailside Park	114		✔		✔			✔	✔
30. Mountain Ranch Estates	116		+					*	✔

✔ = Off leash parks/trails
+ = Dog walker preferred
^Kids = playgrounds, courts, etc.
* = Minimal Off-road
^Wheels = strollers or wheelchairs
* = Smooth but steep
++ = Conditions permitting, snow may be packed down or cleared

#1 City Park - Main Street

Description: If you only take one of the 30 walks in this book, this should be it. You'll experience some of the best recreational, cultural, and culinary delights that Park City has to offer. Expect to spend more time than the distance suggests if you're inclined to read menus, explore galleries and boutiques, take pictures, and/or watch athletes fly around a skate park. Main Street is Park City's most popular tourist attraction.

Main Street frequently stages festivals, parades, concerts, and special events.
Photo by Ken Hurwitz MD

Distance: 3.0 miles (4.8 km)
Elevation Gain: 300 feet (91 m)
Peak Elevation: 7,188 feet (2,192 m)
Difficulty: INTERMEDIATE. Walk up a gentle incline for the first mile and then the free Main Street Trolley becomes an option. Most people are too busy enjoying Main Street's amenities to be bothered by the 1½ miles (2.4 km) it takes to walk it both up and down.
Surface: Paved surfaces except for occasional construction walkways.
Cautions: This popular route may be crowded at peak times. Sidewalks are narrow and many people window-shop. The Poison Creek Trail is a favorite of cyclists, skateboarders, and dog walkers.
Restrooms are available in City Park, south of the Park City Museum on the east side of Main Street, and in Miners Park on the west side.

Notable Features:

- Park City's **City Park** at the north end of Old Town provides playgrounds, sports fields and courts, a five-tier skate park, an amphitheater and picnic facilities. It's also the relocation site of **Miners Hospital**. In the old days, thousands of miners with injuries and "Miners' Con" (consumption of the lungs) were cared for in this facility.

The Miners Hospital lawn in City Park serves as an outdoor gym for exercise classes.

- **Poison Creek Trail** is an artist-decorated paved path from City Park to Old Town. This delightful trail with its unfortunate name borders a stream that was previously polluted by the mining industry and outhouses along its banks.
- **Shoe Tree Park** on the east side of the Poison Creek was built around a tradition that started in the 1960s when some locals flung shoes into a tree. In 2011,

disapproving residents persuaded Park City officials to remove enough footwear to fill 26 big garbage bags, but the trees were quickly redecorated with all kinds of footwear, even ski boots. It seems that Shoe Tree Park has become an ongoing conflict between residents who cherish this custom and less appreciative newcomers. Perhaps the shoes won't be there when your walk, but you can still enjoy a **picnic** park built around the trees.

☒ **Historic Main Street** offers a smorgasbord of restaurants, galleries, exclusive boutiques, and souvenir shops, and hosts the "Silly Market" festival on summer Sundays. Find a calendar of gallery tours and events on the Chamber of Commerce website at www.visitparkcity.com.

☒ **The Park City Museum**, 528 Main Street provides exhibits of the town and life in old Park City, including a mock-up of a mine and an interactive map that shows more than a thousand miles (1609+ km) of mining tunnels beneath the resorts. Tour the **territorial jail** preserved in the museum basement to see the less romantic side of the Old West. Rotating traveling exhibits are featured in the Museum's **Tozer Gallery**. Check www.parkcitymuseum.org/.

The Park City Museum was originally City Hall, built in 1885.

☒ **The Egyptian Theatre,** 328 Main Street, was built in 1926. Egyptian décor became a global fashion with the 1922 discovery of King Tut's 3,000+ year-old intact tomb. (King Tutankhamum ruled Egypt c.1332-1323 BC.)

☒ The **Wasatch Brew Pub**, 250 Main Street, was established in 1986, the first brewery in Utah and one of the first craft brewers in the country. The microbrewery movement started in the UK in the 1970s. Today there are about 3,000 independent craft brewers in the U.S.A.

☒ The **Imperial Hotel** at 221 Main Street was a miners' boarding house in the early 1900s. It was recently renovated to feature a delicatessen.

☒ **Park City Live**, 427 Main Street, occupies the War Veterans Memorial Building, constructed in 1939 with federal funding. This building previously housed Boy Scouts, the American Legion, and a bowling alley. It currently serves as a venue for top name entertainment.

☒ The **Family Tree Visitors Center**, 531 Main Street, enables people to investigate their personal ancestry.

☒ The **Union Pacific Railroad Depot**, (The Depot), 660 Main Street, functioned as a railroad station from 1886 until the mid 1970's. In 1986, the last train rolled out of Park City, after which this building was converted to a restaurant by film icon Robert Redford.

Directions:

* The nearest **bus** stop is at the 7-11 store at the north end of Park Avenue. Behind the store, find a ball field. Take the path alongside the field and it bends

left towards tennis courts.

* **Drivers** should turn south off of Deer Valley Drive and park at the north end of City Park. There's additional parking south in the park if needed. City Park is also accessible by turning east from Park Avenue. Then turn left on Sullivan Road and wind around to park near the tennis courts.

* Start on the paved path that has you passing tennis courts on your left, and come to an intersection with another paved path.

* Turn right heading south on this path, the Poison Creek Trail. Pass sports fields and a skate park.

* At a fork showing Main Street to the right, bear left towards the Lost Prospector Trail.

* At a second fork with a basketball court to the right, bear left again and you will come to another fork showing Deer Valley to the left.

* Bear right here and arrive on Heber Avenue and walk to the crosswalk at the next intersection with Main Street.

* Cross Heber Avenue and you are now on the east side of Main Street. You can walk up or ride the free trolley.

* At the top of Main Street past the Wasatch Brew Pub, cross to the west side to enjoy your downhill walk, re-crossing Heber Avenue and continuing onto lower Main Street. After passing the Town Lift Plaza where a chair lift links ski trails with town, you'll come to a left turn, Ninth Street.

* Turn left onto Ninth and it will quickly bring you around a curve to intersect with Park Avenue.

* Turn right going north on the east sidewalk of Park Avenue. **Bus** riders will be able to get the bus along Park Avenue. **Drivers** should continue to the next corner on the right, Sullivan Road (an extension of 12th Street).

* Turn right onto Sullivan. The sidewalk alternates from the left to the right side of the street around parking. Continue to the tennis courts where you started.

Route Summary:

» Start in the north end of City Park at the tennis courts.

» Take the path alongside of the tennis courts and turn right onto the Poison Creek Trail heading south.

» Bear left at two forks showing Main Street to the right. At a third fork showing Deer Valley to the left, bear right onto Heber Avenue heading west towards Main Street.

» Turn left onto the east side of Main Street.

» At the top of Main, cross the street to descend on the west side.

» Cross Heber Avenue to lower Main Street and continue to Ninth Street.

» Turn left onto Ninth Street.

» Turn right onto Park Avenue to return to the bus stop. Drivers should turn right onto Sullivan Road from Park Avenue and follow it north to the tennis court parking.

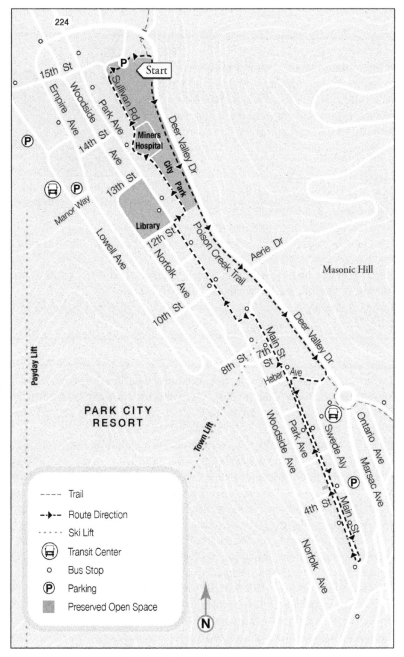

#1 City Park — Main Street

#2 Old Town Via Park City Resort

Description: This ridgeline route is sandwiched between Park Avenue and ski terrain and shows how the resort integrates with the town. A mixture of miner's shacks, gingerbread cottages, A-frames, and contemporary architecture line these residential streets. Some tiny appearing homes are actually quite large, with multiple stories cascading down steep slopes.

Ski trails through Old Town provide great summer hiking.

Distance: 2.2 miles (3.5 km)
Elevation Gain: 302 feet (92 m)
Peak Elevation: 7,325 feet (2,233 m)
Difficulty: DIFFICULT due to a steep incline at the start.
Surface: Mostly paved roads, but they are narrow and have limited shoulders. There's also soft dirt single-track.
Cautions: Vehicular and cyclist traffic. Possible construction. This route is inaccessible during ski season, and snow may last well into spring.
Restrooms are available at the Park City Resort and the library on Park Avenue when open.

Notable Features:

- Towers ascending the mountain near the town chairlift are vestiges of the **Silver King Aerial Tramway**. Built in 1901, it brought ore from the mines into town in flying buckets, and took supplies back to the mines. It cut the cost of transporting ore from $1.50 per ton by horse and wagon to $0.22.

- **Park City Library**, 1255 Park Avenue. Park City's first library was established in the Congregational Church basement in the 1880's. A century later, 750 people passed 5,000 books hand-to-hand for ¾ of a mile (1.2 km) from the library's Main Street location to the Miners Hospital in City Park. The library outgrew that building in the 1990s and was relocated here. Another human chain restocked shelves after a high tech renovation in 2015. Check parkcitylibrary.org/. This 1928 building formerly served as the Park City High School and Carl Winters Middle School, but was outgrown by the school district in 1981. In addition to housing the library, the school auditorium serves as a community theater.

- **Chateau Apres Lodge**, 1299 Norfolk Avenue, was one of the first skier hotels built in conjunction with the opening of Park City Ski Area in the 1960s. It continues to provide dormitory accommodations as well as private guest rooms.

- **Park City Resort** features a multilevel plaza with lodging, dining and shopping. Summer features include an alpine slide, alpine coaster, zip line, scenic lift rides,

lift assisted hiking and cycling, horseback riding, miniature golf, a climbing wall, and other **amusement park** activities. Not all businesses are open all seasons, though most are open during ski season and on summer weekends. See www.parkcity-mountain.com for more information.

Directions:

* **Drive** or take the **bus** to the transit center at the Park City Resort and proceed to the SW corner of the south parking lot, turning left as you exit the bus.

Ride a chairlift, horse, or bicycle if you rather not walk up the mountain or play at the Park City Resort Plaza

* From the intersection of Lowell Avenue and Manor Way, walk south, ascending Lowell Avenue. Continue on Lowell until it becomes a dirt path, just right of a residential driveway as the road bends left.
* Proceed up this steep but short dirt path. Ignore some turnoffs to the right and left. Find a fork at the crest.
* Bear right at the fork (but not extreme right) and you'll be on a tree-lined trail, looking down on the town. The trail ends on Norfolk Avenue. Continue south on Norfolk and after it bends right, arrive at an intersection with King Road.
* Turn left onto King and proceed to the next intersection, Woodside Avenue.
* Turn left onto Woodside and follow it around a right bend where it intersects with Park Avenue. After a rock wall, notice a dirt/gravel footpath to the left.
* Turn left onto the footpath. It takes you past the west end of the ski bridge under the chairlift, crisscrosses a ski trail and then descends to end at the intersection of Crescent Tram and Woodside Avenue.
* Turn left onto Crescent Tram, (Eighth Street), and proceed to the next intersection with Norfolk Avenue.
* Turn right onto Norfolk and proceed north, passing the back of the Park City Library. When you reach the corner of Thirteenth Street, (Calhoun Street), look for a staircase to your left.
* Climb the staircase to Empire Avenue and turn right to arrive back at the **parking** lot and **bus** stop at Park City Resort.

Route Summary:

» Start at the SW corner of the Park City Resort parking lot where Lowell Avenue intersects Manor Way.
» Proceed south on Lowell to the dirt trail just before Lowell bends left. Ascend the steep short trail onto a dirt path.
» Bear right where the path forks and follow this trail until it ends on Upper Norfolk Avenue. Proceed on Norfolk to King Road.
» Turn left onto King and proceed to Woodside Avenue.

» Turn left onto Woodside and continue past a right bend and rock wall to find a footpath on the left.

» Take the footpath under the chairlift and descend to an intersection with Crescent Tram (Eighth Street).

» Turn left onto Crescent Tram and proceed a short way to the corner of Norfolk Avenue.

» Turn right onto Norfolk and pass the library.

» Take the staircase on your left at the intersection of Norfolk and Thirteenth Street. The stairs take you to Empire Avenue.

» Turn right onto Empire to return to start.

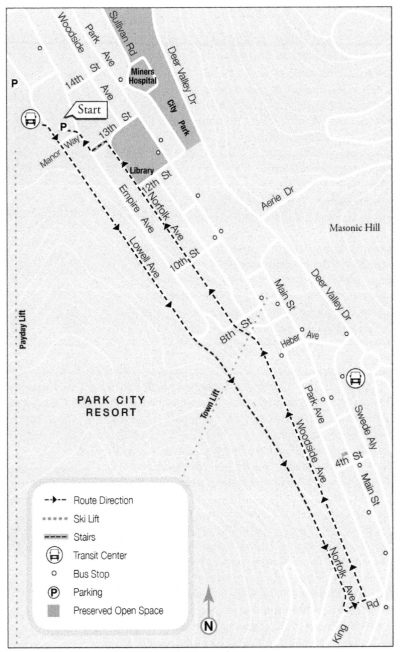

#2 Old Town Via Park City Resort

#3 Empire Avenue - Park Avenue

Description: This walk along narrow residential streets at the foot of Park City Resort is an architect's Disneyland. Intermingled with historic homes and churches, you'll find ultramodern mountain engineering. Some homes built into uphill terrain are accessible only by climbing lengthy stairs. The return loop takes you past many historic addresses.

Distance: 2.9 miles (4.7 km)
Elevation Gain: 352 ft. (107 m)
Highest Elevation: 7,349 feet (2,240 m)
Difficulty: DIFFICULT due to a long steady climb at the start.
Surface: Paved roads but they are narrow and have limited shoulders. Climb 2 staircases.
Cautions: Minimal vehicular and cyclist traffic, and possible construction. It's not recommended for dogs.
Restrooms are available at the Park City Resort and at the library on Park Avenue when open.

Mountain-climb the easy way. This serrated metal Old Town staircase provides great traction in snow, but distress to dog feet.

Notable Features:

- St. Mary's of the Assumption **Catholic Church** and **School**, 121 Park Avenue, built in 1884, was one of the first non-Mormon churches built in Utah. The presence of Catholics, Methodists, Lutherans, Episcopalians, Congregationalists, Jews, Buddhists, and others in Park City in the 1800s, made the town an island of religious diversification in the Mormon dominated region.

- Park City **Community Church**, 402 Park Avenue. A church was built by Congregationalists on this site in 1883, when Park City was little more than a mining camp. It was rebuilt after the Great Fire of 1898, in Gothic style, fashionable in that era. It became a community church in 1919 when several Protestant sects united. The building passed into private hands after a new church was built in Snyderville.

- The **Blue Church**, 424 Park Avenue, was constructed in 1897 as a Mormon meetinghouse, was lost in the Great Fire of 1898, and was rebuilt in 1899. The Mormon congregation moved to bigger quarters in 1962. After housing a dance studio and an art

This Community Church features lancet shaped windows in groups, and pointed (ogival) arches, characteristic of Gothic architecture.

museum, it was converted to condominiums.

෨ St. Luke's **Episcopalian Church**, 525 Park Ave, also Gothic in style, was originally built two blocks south, but was rebuilt here in 1901 after the Great Fire. Restoration in 1978 modernized the interior for current attendees.

With many miners being of Scandinavian origin, St. John's **Lutheran Church** was organized in Park City in 1902. In the mid-1800s, religious fervor and proselytizing in the United States and Europe resulted in Mormon missionaries converting and convincing some freezing Scandinavians that Utah's deserts were divine. Then, Scandinavian missionaries came to Utah to convert their countrymen back to their Lutheran faith, the state religion of Norway and Denmark. As a result, Lutheran churches proliferated in Utah. Park City's Lutheran Church is now in its suburbs. Find more information about **places of worship** at www. visitparkcity.com/members/member-directory/churches-chapels-synagogues.

෨ **Washington School House**, 543 Park Ave, built in 1889, was one of Park City's first schools. From 1936 through the 1950's it was a VFW (Veterans of Foreign Wars) social hall. It opened as the Washington School Inn in 1985, and now operates as a luxury hotel.

෨ **High West Distillery**, 703 Park Ave, a producer of award winning spirits, is also a restaurant and saloon at the bottom of the Quittin' Time ski run. Built in the early 1900s, this building served as a livery stable for horses that pulled heavy carts of ore. With the arrival of the automobile it became a service station from 1915 to 1942. It was a residence before becoming the distillery. Repainted signs on this old building have faded away to what you now see.

෨ As in walk #2, a segment of **Woodside Avenue** is included for this route as it's one of the town's few connector streets. Woodside is steeped both in history and terrain. Some of Park City's wealthiest citizens built homes here in the 1880s.

෨ **Park City Resort** at the start and end of your walk offers dining, shopping and recreational opportunities including winter skiing and **ice skating**, year round mountain **thrill rides** and other activities in summer, as noted in Walk #2.

෨ This walk may take you past the Treasure Hill development on the south side of Park City Resort. This controversial slope-side project has been planned for decades but was not yet underway when this book was written.

Directions:

* **Drive** or take the **bus** to the Park City Resort and proceed to the SE corner of the south parking lot, to your left as you exit the bus.

* From the parking lot, proceed to the intersection of Manor Way and Empire Avenue and head south on Empire Avenue, continuing until it intersects with Crescent Tram, south of Tenth Street on the left.

* Turn left onto Crescent Tram, (8th Street), a winding little road that was once a narrow gauge railroad for transporting silver ore. Proceed to the next intersection with Norfolk Avenue.

* Turn right onto Norfolk and it will appear that you are walking toward a house at the end of a dead end street. To the right of the house, find a step up to a sidewalk. Follow this sidewalk to Woodside Avenue.

* Bearing south on Woodside, you'll pass several long sets of steps going downhill between houses on the left. As you approach the end of the street, notice a crosswalk and a fire hydrant to the right, at the foot of a staircase that goes both up and down. (If you're not game to climb up 117 steps, you can descend the steps here and you'll come out on Park Avenue. Turn left onto Park Avenue and skip to the directions four steps below.) If you ascend the steps, turn left onto Upper Norfolk Avenue at the top.

* Proceed a short distance on Upper Norfolk and you'll come to a right hand turn, Sampson Avenue, which goes off at a diagonal. Don't confuse it with private driveways.

* Turn right onto Sampson and ascend for a short distance; then Sampson rolls downhill and around a switchback. You'll come to a W-intersection with King and Ridge Avenues.

* Take the far left turn onto Ridge Avenue and follow it downhill as it bends into Daly Avenue.

* Turn left onto Daly Avenue. Daly ends at an X-intersection with Main Street veering right. Bear left at the end of Daly onto Park Avenue and continue on Park until you come to Thirteenth Street. (If you're tired, you could take the free Main Street Trolley from the top of Main Street to the Transit Center and then a bus back to the parking lot at Park City Resort, though the walking is mostly downhill from here.) There are 32 historic addresses on Park Avenue.

* For walkers, turn left onto Thirteenth Street, and ascend it heading west to a staircase. Climb up the stairs and turn right at the top to get to the south **parking** lot and **bus** stop at Park City Resort.

Route Summary:

» Start at the SE corner of the south parking lot at Park City Resort.
» Proceed onto Empire Avenue going south.
» Turn left onto Crescent Tram.
» Turn right onto Norfolk Avenue. Proceed to the end.
» Look to the right for a sidewalk to Woodside Avenue.
» Proceed south on Woodside to an up-staircase next to a fire hydrant on your right. Ascend the stairs.
» Turn left onto Upper Norfolk at the top.
» Turn right onto Sampson Avenue and proceed to a W-intersection.
» Take the extreme left turn onto Ridge Avenue.
» Turn left onto Daly Avenue and proceed to the X-intersection.
» Bear left onto Park Avenue at the X.
» Turn left onto Thirteenth Street heading west and ascend a staircase to return to start.

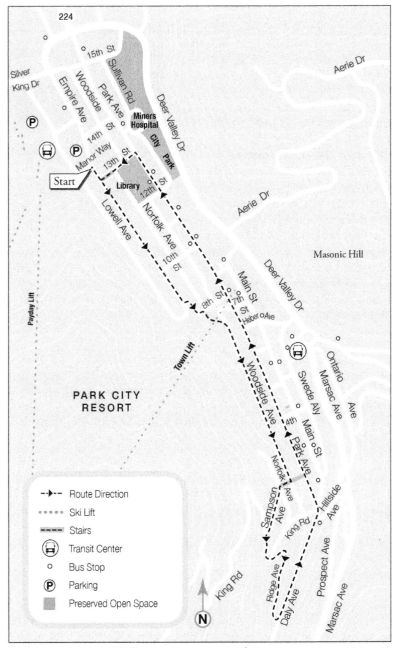

#3 Empire Avenue - Park Avenue

#4 Masonic Hill - Deer Valley

Description: Exceptional views of Park City and ski terrain are available from this ridgeline route that traverses Masonic Hill above Old Town, and takes you through a variety of Deer Valley neighborhoods.

Masonic Hill borders Park City's east side. Some early Mormon leaders were also Freemasons. The closest Masonic lodge is now in Heber City.
Photo by Ken Hurwitz MD

Distance: 1.86 miles (2.93 km)
Elevation Gain: 155 feet (47 m)
Peak Elevation: 7,204 feet (2196 m)
Difficulty: INTERMEDIATE due to some short but steep inclines and single-track. You can tackle the steep part at the beginning if you come by bus or at the end if you come by car.
Surface: Paved roads and paths and a single-track trail that begins with a short but mildly rocky incline.
Cautions: Vehicular and cyclist traffic. Be especially cautious crossing Deer Valley Drive and the roundabout crosswalks.
Restrooms are not available along this route but are nearby on Main Street, or detour to Deer Valley Plaza.

Notable Features:

⌇ The **Lost Prospector Trail** represents the well-maintained trail system and provides trail connections, and the **Poison Creek Trail** provides another perspective on Shoe Tree Park, noted in Walk #1.

⌇ Detour to Deer Valley to enjoy the **duck ponds** of Walk #6, hiking, or resort amenities.

Directions:

✳ Take the **bus** to the intersection of Main and Ninth Streets and walk east on Main Street to Deer Valley Drive.

✳ Turn left and walk north along Deer Valley Drive until you see an uphill road across the street. Carefully, cross Deer Valley Drive, and proceed onto Aerie Drive.

✳ If **driving**, turn east off of Deer Valley Drive onto Aerie Drive and find limited parking immediately to the right. If unavailable, park along Swede Alley in Old Town and walk back.

✳ The Lost Prospector Trail is on both sides of the road. Ascend to the trail on the south (right) side and proceed up a short, steep single-track until you come to a double-track.

* Turn left onto the double-track.
* Quickly turn right at the next intersecting single-track. Proceed along this trail, passing below a water tank and crossing a dirt road, after which the trail bends right and ends on Mellow Mountain Road.
* Continue downhill, cautiously on the curves of Mellow Mountain Road, to an intersection with Sunnyside Drive.
* Turn right onto Sunnyside, and proceed downhill to Deer Valley Drive. (If you continue on Mellow Mountain, you'll arrive at Deer Valley Drive closer to the resort and duck ponds.)
* Cross Deer Valley Drive, turn right and follow the sidewalk downhill to a roundabout.
* Carefully cross at crosswalks three times in the roundabout. Then bear right and quickly turn left to go north on the Poison Creek Trail.
* Look for a fire hydrant next to a staircase on the left, after passing Shoe Tree Park. Ascend the stairs onto a plaza with a ramp to Main Street, which bends right.
* **Bus** riders should turn left onto Main Street and follow it to an intersection with Ninth Street and the bus stop.
* **Drivers** should turn right, cross Main Street, proceed to its NE corner, and turn left. Then, proceed carefully along Deer Valley Drive and cross it to ascend Aerie Drive to your car.

Route Summary:

» Start on Aerie Drive at the trailhead for the Lost Prospector Trail on the south side of the road.
» Turn right onto this single-track and proceed to an intersection with a double-track trail.
» Turn left onto the double-track and quickly turn right, back onto single-track. Follow it to Mellow Mountain Road.
» Proceed downhill on Mellow Mountain.
» Turn right onto Sunnyside Drive and proceed to the end.
» Cross Deer Valley Drive, turn right and proceed downhill.
» Proceed through three crosswalks at the roundabout.
» Bear right out of the roundabout and then quickly turn left onto the Poison Creek Trail.
» Leave the Poison Creek Trail ascending stairs by a fire hydrant, after Shoe Tree Park.
» Bus riders turn left onto Main Street and follow it to the Main and Ninth Streets bus stop. Drivers turn right, cross Main Street and proceed to Deer Valley Drive.
» Turn left onto Deer Valley Drive and cross it at the intersection with Aerie Drive to return to the car.

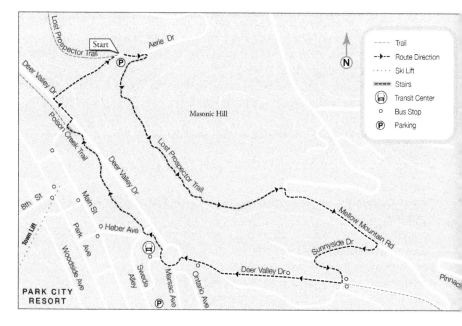

	Trail
	Route Direction
	Ski Lift
	Stairs
Ⓗ	Transit Center
o	Bus Stop
Ⓟ	Parking

#4 Masonic Hill - Deer Valley

#5 Ontario Ridge - Rossie Hill

Description: This route starts and ends in old neighborhoods in Old Town, takes you onto ridgeline trails through mossy woodlands, and offers peeks into Park City's unpolished past.

Oh, the tales it could tell if this Ontario Ridge relic could talk! Photo by Ken Hurwitz MD

Distance: 2.5 miles (4 km)
Elevation Gain: 397 feet (121 m)
Highest Elevation: 7,586 feet (2312 m)
Difficulty: DIFFICULT due to a steep ascent for the first ¼ mile (0.4 km) and some narrow single-track.
Surface: Mostly single-track with some pavement and staircases mixed in.
Cautions: Cyclist and vehicular traffic, and one serious road crossing.
Restrooms are not available along this route but can be found in public facilities in Old Town (see Walk #1).

Notable Features:

- Prospect Avenue features some interesting **historic** residences.
- Vestiges of old Park City are found along the **Prospect Trail** on Ontario Ridge, purchased by Park City Municipal for trail preservation.
- **Trail connections** are available.

Directions:

* **Bus** riders take the Main Street Trolley south to the turnaround where Main Street intersects with Hillside Avenue. Proceed east, ascending Hillside to Prospect Avenue and turn right on Prospect.
* **Drivers** can park in the Sandridge two-tiered parking lots, accessible from Deer Valley Drive at the south end of Old Town. Find a sidewalk in the SW corner of the upper parking lot and follow it to Hillside Avenue. Cross Hillside and proceed up steep Prospect Avenue.
* Proceed onto a dirt trail where the Prospect pavement ends. Follow this dirt path to a three-pronged fork and take the middle branch.
* Arrive at a second fork and take the left branch that descends on a narrow trail from Ontario Ridge to Marsac Avenue.
* Carefully cross Marsac and turn right. Pass a steep gravel road up the next ridge and quickly find a dirt path to your left, the Rossie Hill Trail.
* Turn sharply left onto this trail and follow it as it bends right. Ignore a left switchback and a right fork. Arrive at a double-track dirt road.
* Turn left onto this road and come to an intersection of multiple trails. Take the

trail to the right, passing two low boulders to your left.

* Ignore the first right turn and take the second right turn onto another single-track, which ends on a cul-de-sac, McHenry Avenue.

* Walk north on McHenry to a long staircase on the left.

* Descend the stairs and turn right onto Ontario Avenue. Walk north on Ontario to another long staircase on the left.

* Descend these stairs to Marsac Avenue. Cross Marsac at a crosswalk and take a few steps down and turn left onto a sidewalk that circles a pocket park. **Bus/trolley** riders can follow the pocket park path to the right to Swede Alley, and turn right on Swede Alley to get to the transit center, (shown on map #4).

* If you **drove**, take the circular sidewalk to the left to a staircase to the lower Sandridge parking. There are more stairs to the upper lot.

Route Summary:

» Start at Prospect Avenue, just east of Rt. 224 south of Old Town.

» Ascend Prospect Avenue and continue onto the Prospect Trail.

» At a three-pronged fork, take the middle branch.

» Bear left at a 2nd fork onto a narrow trail down to Marsac Avenue.

» Cross Marsac, turn right, pass a steep gravel road and turn sharply left onto single-track. Ignore a left switchback and a right fork.

» Come to a double-track road. Turn left and come to an intersection.

» Bear right at the intersection, passing low boulders to the left.

» Pass a right turn and turn right at a second intersecting trail. Follow it to a cul-de-sac and continue on the street to a staircase to the left.

» Take the stairs down to Ontario Avenue, turn right, and proceed to the next staircase on the left.

» Take the stairs down to Marsac Avenue and cross it. Descend a few more stairs and turn left onto a circular sidewalk. Bus/trolley riders bear right to Swede Alley, turn right, and proceed to the transit center.

» Drivers should bear left and the circular sidewalk arrives at a staircase that ascends to the Sandridge parking lots.

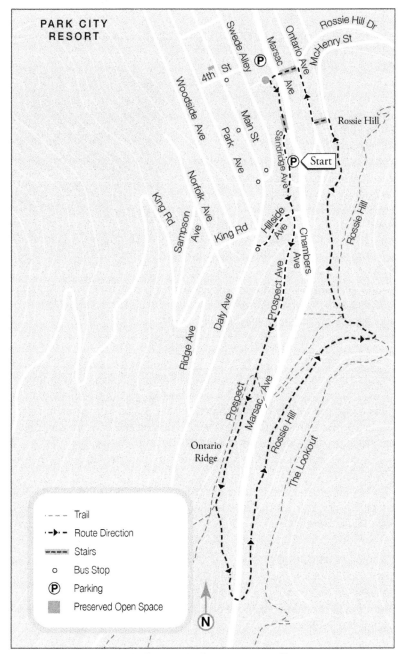

#6 Deer Valley Duck Ponds

Description: Enjoy a maze of footpaths meandering around ponds and residences in a park like setting at the foot of Deer Valley Resort.

Distance: You can take a variety of loops varying from about 1 to 1.5 miles (1.6-2.4 km)
Elevation Gain: 46 feet (14 m)
Peak Elevation: 7,203 feet (21.95m)
Difficulty: EASY walking on level terrain.
Surface: Pavement, wooden bridges, and dirt or gravel paths. Wheelchairs can find paved options around the periphery.
Cautions: Dogs are not welcome along some residential portions of these trails, but dog walkers frequent most of these paths. Just heed signs.
Restrooms are available at the Deer Valley Plaza at the SW corner of the ponds, and seasonally, at Snow Park Lodge at Deer Valley Resort.

Deer Valley isn't actually a town. It's a Park City subdivision with awesome amenities like a ski resort and duck ponds.

Notable Features:

- **Wildlife** may come for a drink at dusk and dawn. You can watch from a gazebo within this refuge. It's an ideal place for **birding**
- Take a side trip to ride the **free funicular**, SW of the entry plaza to Deer Valley Resort. Views from the funicular are outstanding and you can walk back down by picking up trails described in Walk #7.
- These short walks around the duck ponds are easily combined with Walks #4, #7, #8 or #9.
- Dining and spa options may be available. Summer activities include **historical guided tours** and special events. Find information at www.deervalley.com/WhatToDo/Summer.

Directions (Route Summary):

- Take the **bus** to any bus stop along Deer Valley Drive East or North.
- **Drivers** can find parking east of the ponds in the resort lots.
- Have fun in the maze. You'll always come out on Deer Valley Drive near a bus stop if you get disoriented.

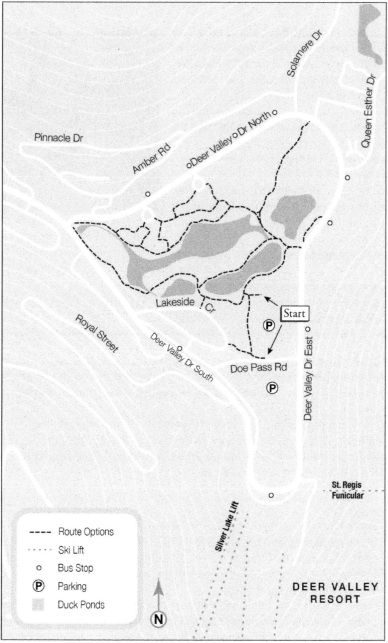

Pinnacle Dr

Solamere Dr

Queen Esther Dr

Amber Rd

Deer Valley Dr North

Lakeside Cr

Start

Royal Street

Deer Valley Dr South

Doe Pass Rd

Deer Valley Dr East

St. Regis
Funicular

Silver Lake Lift

Route Options
Ski Lift
Bus Stop
Parking
Duck Ponds

N

DEER VALLEY
RESORT

#6 Deer Valley Duck Ponds

#7 Deer Valley - Deer Crest

Description: This walk takes you along a Deer Valley ski slope and through a resort neighborhood with views of the Jordanelle Reservoir. Riding the St. Regis Funicular can eliminate most of the uphill walking.

Take a free ride on the Swiss-made funicular. Photo by Ken Hurwitz MD

Distance: 2.5 miles (4 km) if you don't take the funicular, 1.8 miles (2.9 km) if you do.
Elevation Gain: 394 feet (120 m) for walkers
Peak Elevation: 7,508 feet (2,288 m)
Difficulty: EASY or DIFFICULT, depending on use of the funicular. Some uphill walking is required of drivers, but bus riders have a no-uphill option.
Surface: Pavement, single-track trails and stairs.
Cautions: Minimal vehicular or cyclist traffic.
Restrooms may be available at Snow Park Lodge at the base of Deer Valley Resort, seasonally, or at Deer Valley Plaza, SW of the resort.

Notable Features:

- A free **funicular** ride from the Deer Valley parking area to the St. Regis Deer Valley Resort takes you uphill and provides great views. You can also ride it back down.
- Dining and spa options, and special events take place at the **resorts**.
- There are numerous **trail options** at Deer Valley Resort. Maps can be found at www.deervalley.com/WhatToDo/Summer or at businesses around the resort. Find the Duck Pond map in Walk #6.

Directions:

- Take the **bus** to the Deer Valley Resort base.
- The resort **parking** and bus stop allow close access to the funicular, east of the resort base. If you park near the funicular, some uphill walking comes at the end of the route. Parking in the NE corner of the lots will have you walking uphill to start with less uphill at the end.
- From the parking or bus stop, follow the road that ascends to the funicular building. Enter the building, and ascend to the second floor by stairs or elevator. Push the button and a car will arrive shortly if not there. On top, exit the building to the SE, opposite the duck ponds.

* To walk instead of ride, look for Finn's Trail to your left, as soon as you turn onto the road to the funicular building.
* Turn left onto Finn's Trail and follow it to an intersection where you'll turn right at a switchback.
* Come to a T-intersection and turn left.
* Turn right at the third intersection (switchback) to merge with the St. Regis Connector Trail.
* At a fourth intersection turn right. Cross under the funicular.
* From the upper funicular building, bear south around the building and follow around the resort pools onto a ski slope. As the slope descends under a road, bear left and ascend a few steps up to the resort plaza.
* Turn right and follow the plaza around the periphery of the resort to a staircase. Descend these stairs and turn left onto the road, Deer Crest Estates Drive.
* Proceed downhill on Deer Crest until you come to gates that allow pedestrian passage around the sides.
* Arrive at a second set of gates after a short distance. Take the passage way around either side. Follow a dirt path to Queen Esther Drive.
* Turn left on Queen Esther and proceed to Deer Valley Drive East.
* Turn left on Deer Valley Drive East and proceed to the **bus** stop or to where you **parked.**

Route Summary:

» Start at the east end of the Deer Valley Resort base where a road ascends to a funicular building for the option of an uphill lift.
» Turn left onto Finn's Trail at the start of the road to the funicular.
» Walking up Finn's trail, you'll come to four intersections. Turn right at the first, left at the second, and turn right at the third and fourth.
» From the funicular building bear left around the resort pools, arriving at a three-step staircase.
» Take the stairs to a plaza and bear right to a down staircase.
» Descend the stairs and turn left, heading north onto Deer Crest Estates Drive. Pass around two sets of gates to descend onto a dirt path that ends on Queen Esther Drive.
» Turn left on Queen Esther and proceed to Deer Valley Drive East.
» Turn left onto Deer Valley Drive to return to parking or the bus.

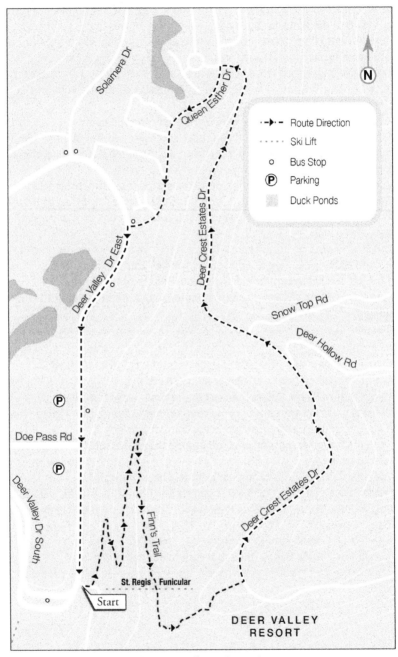

#7 Deer Valley - Deer Crest

#8 Silver Lake Village

Description: This is a short, easy walk amidst the glitz and glamour of Deer Valley Resort. Seasonal chair lift access provides additional options.

Deer Valley is as famous for summer cycling and hiking as it is for great skiing.

Distance: 1.2 miles (1.9 km)
Elevation Gain: 43 feet (13 m)
Peak Elevation: 8,175 feet (2,492 m)
Difficulty: EASY. Inclines are gentle.
Surface: Sidewalk and paved roads.
Cautions: This is the **highest altitude** walk in this book.
Restrooms may be available seasonally in the Silver Lake Lodge.

Notable Features:

- **Silver Lake Village** is the midsection of Deer Valley Resort. Stores, restaurants, and chairlifts are open primarily in winter and summer. Cyclists careening down steep ski slopes entertain the summer lunch crowd.
- Woodland View Drive passes through a **mountain pine forest** where mansions capture exceptional views.
- Resort summer activities include concerts, special events, access to numerous **trails,** and chairlift rides to higher elevations. See www.deervalley.com for more information.

Directions (Route Summary):

* There's **bus** service to Silver Lake only during summer and ski seasons. Take the bus to the stop at the Chateaux. **Drivers** should take Deer Valley Drive to Royal Street to Silver Lake. Free limited parking is available except during ski season or special events. Walking up to Silver Lake is not recommended due to a lack of shoulders on winding roads.
* From the bus stop or parking, head east onto Royal Street East. It bends left and takes you past Sterling Drive to Woodland View Drive.
* Turn left on Woodland View and follow it to Royal Street.
* Turn left on Royal Street, cross to the sidewalk, and follow it back to the **bus** stop or **parking**.

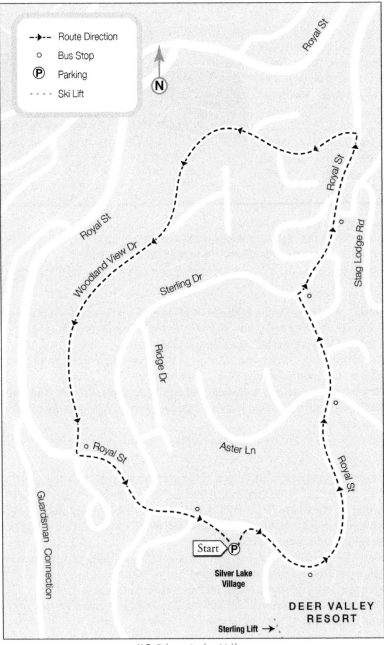

Route Direction
Bus Stop
Parking
Ski Lift

N

Royal St

Woodland View Dr

Sterling Dr

Ridge Dr

Aster Ln

Royal St

Stag Lodge Rd

Guardsman Connection

Royal St

Start P

Silver Lake
Village

**DEER VALLEY
RESORT**

Sterling Lift →

#8 Silver Lake Village

#9 Lower and Upper Deer Valley

Description: This is a somewhat challenging walk that takes you past opulent residences with outrageous views in the Deer Valley suburbs. While you are gaping at the CEO's ski castle, the CEO could be sailing on his yacht in Puget Sound, riding horses on his Montana ranch, or sleeping in his Paris apartment. Still, it is the natural beauty of this neighborhood that is most enviable.

Neighborhood walks are a great spring option when mountain trails are still snowy.

Distance: 4.8 miles (7.7 km)
Elevation Gain: 387 feet (186 m)
Peak Elevation: 7,402 feet or (2,256 m)
Difficulty: INTERMEDIATE. Although you'll climb for considerable distance, the inclines are gentle.
Surface: This walk can be done completely on pavement but directions are given for some off-road paths.
Cautions: Auto traffic during ski season or concerts.
Restrooms can only be found at the start and end of this loop at Deer Valley Plaza, or seasonally at Snow Park Lodge.

Notable Features:

- Outstanding **views** will greet you going and coming. Homes are set in parks with pedestrian paths and ponds, and along mountain ridges.
- This walk is easily **combined** with the duck ponds of Walk #6.
- Dining and spa options may be available seasonally at the resorts and at Deer Valley Plaza year round.

Directions:

* **Bus** service will take you to the corner of Deer Valley Drive East and Queen Esther Drive. **Drivers** may park in the NE corner of the northern resort parking lot. Then proceed north on Deer Valley Drive East to Queen Esther Drive.
* Turn right onto Queen Esther and follow it around to Telemark Drive.
* Turn right on Telemark and ascend to Thistle Street.
* Turn right on Thistle and proceed to Sunridge Drive.
* Turn right on Sunridge and proceed to Hidden Oaks Lane.
* Turn left on Hidden Oaks and proceed to Solamere Drive.
* Turn left on Solamere and follow it around to a left turn marked "Northern

Entrance to Telemark Drive" and turn left. (To avoid unpaved walking, do not take the entrance to Telemark but continue down Solamere to Deer Valley Drive and take the bus, or turn left to return to the parking lot.)

* If you turned left on Telemark, proceed a short way and you will see a gravel path on the right.

* Turn right onto this path, which will turn to sidewalk. Continue to follow it around tennis courts. You will come to a fork near a pond.

* Take either of the paths that follow around the pond and they'll take you back to Queen Esther Drive.

* Turn right on Queen Esther and proceed to Deer Valley Drive to return to the **bus,** or turn left to return to the **parking**.

Route Summary:

» Start at the corner of Deer Valley Drive East and Queen Esther Drive, turning right onto Queen Esther.

» Turn right on Telemark Drive.

» Turn right on Thistle Street.

» Turn right on Sundridge Drive.

» Turn left on Hidden Oaks Lane.

» Turn left on Solamere Drive.

» Turn left to the "Northern Entrance to Telemark Drive".

» Turn right onto a gravel path. It becomes sidewalk which you should follow until you come to a fork at a pond.

» Take either of the paths around the pond to Queen Esther Drive.

» Turn right to return to the bus. Drivers turn left onto Deer Valley Drive to return to parking.

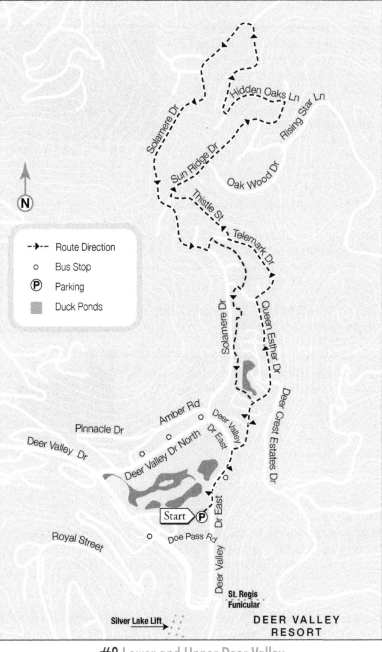

#9 Lower and Upper Deer Valley

#10 Tour of the Tunnels and Rail Trail

Description: This walk traverses three artist-decorated tunnels and takes you along the Union Pacific Rail Trail and Iron Horse District, blending the feel of the Old West with modern-day Park City.

Combine your walk with the insight, imagination, and inspiration of tunnel art.

Distance: 3.0 miles (4.8 km)
Elevation Gain: 210 feet (64m)
Peak Elevation: 6,924 feet (2,110 m)
Difficulty: EASY with relatively level terrain, accessible to wheelchairs.
Surface: All pavement with ramps as needed.
Cautions: Cyclists, especially in tunnels, and road crossings.
Restrooms are available at the school ball fields as described in the directions, and south of the ball fields in City Park.

Notable Features:

- **City Park** provides playgrounds, sports fields and courts, a skate park, and picnic and other facilities. (See Walk #1)
- The **Union Pacific Rail Trail** is a state park stretching 28 miles (45 km) from Park City north to Echo. It borders Silver Creek for 14 miles (22.5 km), and passes through a volcanic canyon and an excavation site for Ice Age artifacts. Along the way find **trail connections** and 16 plaques commemorating early settlers.

Rail Central is reminiscent of Park City's formerly busy train station.

- Note **mirrors** at the ends of some tunnels. Coming from bright light wearing sunglasses, cyclists may not see you, so you have to watch for them.
- **New Prospector Park** at the corner of Comstock Road and Sidewinder Drive features an arch-climbing boulder and fountains.
- Dining and shopping options are found in the Iron Horse District.

Directions:

- ✱ **Bus** riders exit at the 7-11 bus stop on Park Avenue. Behind the store, find a path along side of ball fields that leads to tennis courts.
- ✱ **Drivers** turn south off of Deer Valley Drive into City Park and park near the

tennis courts.

* Take the paved path right of the tennis courts to the next paved path.
* Turn left onto this path, the Poison Creek Trail, and follow it through a short and then a longer tunnel.
* Turn right onto the blacktop path just before a clock tower, the Rail Trail. Proceed about 2/3 of a mile (1.06 km) to the Kearns Bike Path.
* Turn left onto the Kearns Bike Path and follow it through a parking lot to Sidewinder Drive. New Prospector Park is on your right.
* Cross Sidewinder and continue north on the sidewalk along Comstock Road to a traffic light at Kearns Boulevard. To your right are stairs and a ramp to a tunnel that takes you under Kearns.
* Bear left out of the underpass and follow the sidewalk as it jigs around a road divider. Continue along Kearns Boulevard passing the schools. (Just east of the high school parking is a path to a ball field and a small building with public restrooms.) Continue west along Kearns until you come to the intersection of Kearns, Monitor, and Bonanza Drives.
* Using pedestrian crosswalks, first cross Monitor and then Kearns.
* Along Bonanza Drive, follow the sidewalk behind a cauldron sculpture. It crosses Iron Horse Drive and merges with the Poison Creek Trail back to City Park.
* Turn right past the tennis courts to arrive back at the **parking. Bus** riders turn left after passing the tennis courts and then turn right to return to the bus stop in front of the 7-11 store.

Route Summary:

» Start on a path in the north end of City Park.
» Pass tennis courts on your left and turn left onto the next path.
» Proceed through two tunnels.
» Turn right onto the Rail Trail and proceed about 2/3 mile (1.06 km).
» Turn left onto the Kearns Bike Path, cross Sidewinder Drive and proceed north on Comstock Road.
» Cross under Kearns Boulevard and bear left coming out of the tunnel. Follow the sidewalk along Kearns Boulevard to Monitor Drive.
» Cross Monitor Drive and then cross Kearns Boulevard.
» Follow the sidewalk on the west side of Bonanza. It crosses Iron Horse Drive and merges with the Poison Creek Trail.
» Proceed to City Park and turn right after the tennis courts to return to start.

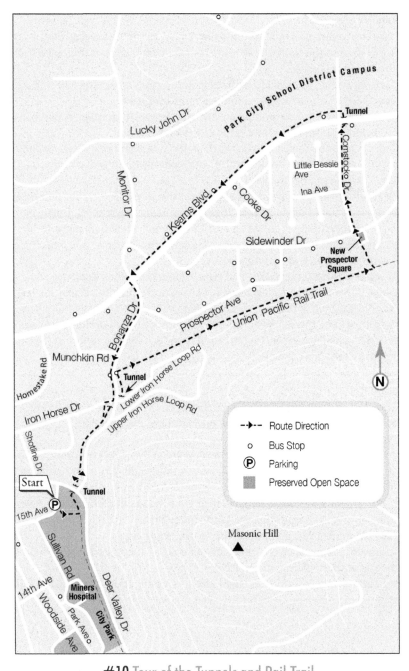

#10 Tour of the Tunnels and Rail Trail

#11 Olympic Plaza - Kearns Boulevard

Description: This suburban route takes you from Olympic glory to the ball fields of the public school campus where future Olympians may be starting their careers. More than 60 U.S.A. athletes competing in the 2014 Sochi Olympics lived or trained in Park City. This route also provides a poignant and momentous view of local history.

Gold, silver, and bronze podium photo-ops are available at the Olympic Welcome Plaza.

Distance: 2.9 miles (4.7 km)
Elevation Gain: 98 feet (30 m)
Peak Elevation: 6,838 feet (2084 m)
Difficulty: This is an EASY level walk.
Surface: All paved except for a few steps on a dirt footpath.
Cautions: Cyclists, road crossings, and possibly errant baseballs.
Restrooms are accessible at businesses in the Snow Creek shopping plaza, and alongside the high school ball fields.

Notable Features:

- **Olympic Welcome Plaza.** This pocket park gives tribute to athletes of the 2002 Salt Lake City Olympics, and to Olympic Game venues around the world.
- **Park City Cemetery** was established in the latter 1800s when the first settlers buried their daughter, Pearl Snyder. Also interred here is Rachel Urban. (Read about this infamous madam in "Park City's Colorful Past.") A gazebo provides shade, seating, and a map to sections for firefighters, veterans, and other congregations. The headstone in this picture leaves little doubt that some in repose here would be eternally happy to see their perpetual mountain view.
- Around the **school campus**, note full-sized and small baseball fields, a softball field, a turf field that triples for football, soccer and lacrosse, a track, and a playground.
- Find **connecting paths** around the Treasure Mountain Junior High where there are additional ball fields, a creek, and a woodchip path accessing wetlands as noted in Walk #18.

Memorial art arose along with public cemeteries in the 19th century.

- Dining and shopping options along south Kearns Boulevard. At the entry to the Holiday Village shopping plaza, a **commemorative bell** offers a historical vignette of the lives of early settlers.
- The boulevard was named after **Thomas Kearns**, who started out as a mucker in 1883 and studied geology at night. He discovered rich veins of ore and became an owner of the lucrative Silver King Mine. In addition to becoming a banking, railroad and newspaper magnate, he served as a Utah United States senator (1901-05).

Directions:

- * Take the bus or drive to the Snow Creek shopping plaza on the NE corner of the intersection of Park Avenue (Rt. 224) and Kearns Boulevard (Rt. 248). There's a **bus** stop south of the Utah State Liquor Store, or **park** on the east side of the liquor store.
- * Cross the street behind the liquor store and to your immediate left is a sidewalk that will take you into the Olympic Welcome Plaza.
- * Exit the Olympic Plaza the same way you came in and make a right turn onto the sidewalk going east. Cross a plaza entry road and continue along Kearns Boulevard, passing commercial and residential areas. The Park City Cemetery fence will appear on your left.
- * Turn left into the first cemetery gate and follow the paths taking left turns at intersections. Hopefully, you are not avoidant of cemeteries; they provide insight into the history of a place and its people that you could not otherwise obtain. You can however, walk alongside the cemetery by staying on the Kearns Boulevard sidewalk. If you've come through the cemetery, you'll ultimately arrive at a dirt footpath left of the cemetery fence that takes you to Monitor Drive.
- * Turn right onto Monitor and proceed to the traffic light. Cross Monitor and continue east along Kearns. Pass the high school and Eccles Center parking lots. Continue on the sidewalk as it jigs left and right around parking, and becomes blacktop heading to the ball fields. (Restrooms are available in the small building between the ball fields.) Past the restrooms, the sidewalk turns right and continues into the parking lot of McPolin Elementary School.
- * Turn left into the parking lot next to a playground and immediately turn left again onto blacktop that goes behind the high school. You'll be heading west alongside of Lucky John Drive, with which the path will merge. Continue on Lucky John Drive to Monitor Drive.
- * Turn left onto Monitor and continue south to the traffic light. You now have 3 options: (1) You can cross Monitor and go back through the cemetery. (2) You can cross Monitor and head west alongside the cemetery, or (3) you can cross Kearns and turn right onto the sidewalk along the south side of Kearns, where you'll have dining and shopping options. This is the recommended route, but you'll need to cross Kearns again at the T-intersection of routes 224 and 248. Then immediately turn right onto the sidewalk, and left onto an intersecting sidewalk into the Olympic Welcome Plaza.
- * Follow the north sidewalk out of the Olympic Plaza to return to **parking** or the **bus** stop.

Route Summary:

» Start at the Olympic Welcome Plaza in the SW corner of the Snow Creek shopping plaza and exit the Olympic Plaza the way you came in.

» Turn right and follow the sidewalk to the first gate of the cemetery.

» Turn left into the cemetery and follow paths taking left turns until you come to a dirt road just north of the cemetery fence.

» Exit the cemetery and turn right onto Monitor Drive.

» Proceed south on Monitor to the traffic light, cross Monitor and follow the sidewalk along Kearns going east, around the Park City High School and its parking.

» Look for a sidewalk at the playground of the McPolin Elementary School. Turn left onto this sidewalk and it will merge with Lucky John Drive. Proceed west on Lucky John to Monitor Drive.

» Turn left onto Monitor and proceed to the traffic light. At the light, cross to the south side of Kearns and turn right, following the paved path going west to the T-intersection of Rt. 224 and Kearns Boulevard.

» Cross to the north side of Kearns at the crosswalk and immediately to your right is an intersecting sidewalk into the Olympic Plaza.

» Exit the plaza on its north side to return to start.

#11 Olympic Plaza - Kearn's Boulevard

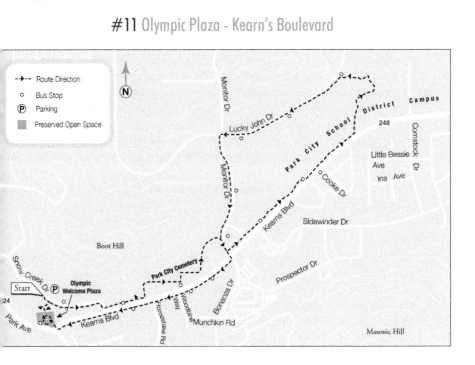

#12 Boot Hill - McLeod Creek

Description: Just behind the Snow Creek shopping plaza is a little hill with low vegetation and big views. You can climb over Boot Hill on your way to shop or dine. This short route also takes you on a paved trail through protected wetlands.

Boot Hill provides easy access and rewarding views.

Distance: 1 mile (1.6 km)
Elevation Gain: 31 feet (9.4 m)
Peak Elevation: 6,854 feet (2,089 m)
Difficulty: INTERMEDIATE due to a moderately steep start.
Surface: A single-track gravel road with ribbons of old asphalt leads to a dirt road and pavement.
Cautions: Minimal cyclist and vehicular traffic. Follow directions; intersecting trails lead to private property.
Restrooms are available at some businesses in the Snow Creek plaza. Mutt-mitts may be available at the start.

Notable Features:

~ The **views** of Park City and Deer Valley Resorts from Boot Hill are grand. This is a perfect perch for watching **sunsets** and still having adequate light to descend.

~ The paved path along the **McLeod** (pronounced ma-cloud) **Creek Trail** goes through some sensitive areas with beaver activity. Beaver dams filter out pollution, and this stream has been designated as a permanent riparian buffer to help preserve water quality. McLeod Creek feeds into the Weber River Watershed, providing drinking water for municipalities from Bountiful to Ogden and beyond.

~ You can detour to see the **Olympic Welcome Plaza**, featured in Walk #11, with which this short walk is easily combined.

Directions:

* Take the **bus** to or **park** in the Snow Creek plaza on the NE corner of the intersection of Park Avenue (Rt. 224), and Kearns Boulevard (Rt. 248).

* From the NE corner of the parking lot, cross the road towards Zions Bank and turn left onto a sidewalk. At the end of the sidewalk turn left onto a gravel road and proceed through a horseshoe bend to the left, another to the right and a third to the left. Continue for about ¼ mile (0.4 km) to a fork, at the NW corner of the big building below you.

* Bear left at the fork and follow this path until it ends on blacktop.
* Turn right onto the blacktop path and make an immediate left onto Saddle View Way, descending amidst townhomes to Windrift Lane.
* Turn left onto a path on the west side of Windrift, bordering an office park. This is the McLeod Creek Trail that takes you back to the west side of the Snow Creek plaza and bus stop.
* When you reach the shopping plaza, **drivers** should turn left, which enables window-shopping on the way back to the car in the plaza's NE corner. **Bus** riders should walk south past the Key Bank to find a sidewalk that leads to the bus stop across from the Olympic Plaza.

Route Summary:

» Start at the sidewalk east of the stores at the NE corner of the Snow Creek plaza. It becomes a gravel path.
» Continue on this path through 3 switchbacks to a fork.
» Bear left at the fork and follow this path to a blacktop path.
» Turn right onto the path and immediately turn left onto Saddle View Way. Proceed to Windrift Lane.
» Turn left onto the paved path west of Windrift, the McLeod Creek Trail. It will take you back to the Snow Creek shopping plaza at its NW end. Drivers started at the NE end. The bus stop is behind (south of) the liquor store.

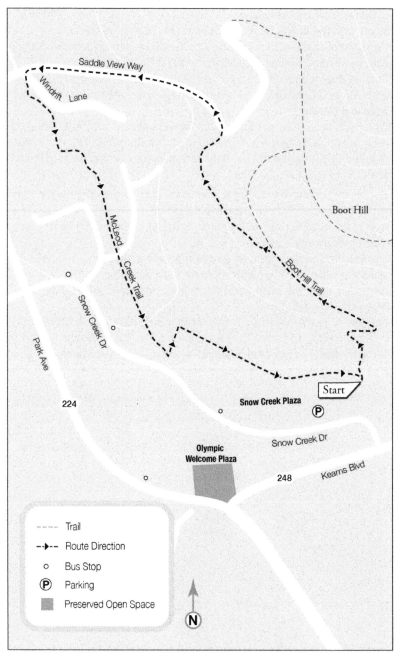

#12 Boot Hill - McLeod Creek Trail

#13 Chatham Hills - Prospector Square

Description: This walk takes you from the historic Rail Trail into a mountain neighborhood, and through Prospector Square, a Park City suburb with resorts, residences, restaurants, and businesses connected by pedestrian walkways.

Distance: 2.33 miles (3.7 km)
Elevation Gain: 318 feet (97 m)
Peak Elevation: 7,006 feet (2,135 m)
Difficulty: INTERMEDIATE due to a moderately steep climb for about 1/3 of a mile (0.5 km).
Surface: Mostly pavement with a few steps on dirt footpaths.
Cautions: Minimal vehicular traffic, some road crossings, and cyclist or skier traffic on the Rail Trail.

Cars rob humans of fitness, clean air, and socialization. Pedestrian friendly communities are the future.
Photo by Ken Hurwitz MD

Restrooms may be accessible in some businesses in Prospector Square.

Notable Features:

~ This route briefly follows the **Union Pacific Rail Trail**, introduced in Walk #10. The Rail Trail is especially popular for **winter walking.** Trail condition reports accompany morning news on local radio station KPCW, 91.7 FM. Or, check the website of the nonprofit Mountain Trails Foundation at mountaintrails.org/conditions/.

~ On a clear day, Chatham Hills provide great **views** of the northern landscape all the way to Ogden.

~ The Prospector Square neighborhood offers multiple amenities including dining. Local street names like Annie Oakley, Wyatt Earp, Buffalo Bill and Doc Holiday honor legendary western Americans from the mid 19th century.

Directions:

✳ On Prospector Avenue there's a bus stop directly across from **parking** lot G. At the SW corner of the parking lot find a footpath to the Rail Trail.

✳ Turn left onto the Rail Trail and proceed east for about 0.7 miles (1.13 km). Look for a sign for the Gambel Oak Trail and a dirt footpath on the right.

✳ Turn right onto the footpath and you'll quickly cross Paddington Drive. Continue straight onto Euston Drive, walking uphill.

✳ Just before Euston Drive ends, turn right onto Paddington Drive, continuing uphill until you come to High Street.

✳ Turn left onto High Street and follow it around a horseshoe and back to Paddington.

✳ Turn left onto Paddington and continue downhill until the road bends right. Look for a footpath straight ahead before the bend.

* Take this short footpath and arrive back on the Rail Trail.
* Turn left onto the Rail Trail and quickly come to a right turn marked Kearns Bike Path and other designations.
* Turn right onto this path. Pass storage facilities and come out in a parking lot. Look for a sidewalk to the left between buildings. Turn left onto this sidewalk crossing through more parking lots, Gold Dust Lane and Poison Creek Lane. Continue past the Silver Mountain Sports Club and into a plaza with restaurants. Continue on the sidewalk as it bends left and arrives back on Prospector Avenue near the bus stop and parking lot G where you started.

Route Summary:

» From parking lot G on Prospector Avenue turn left onto the Rail Trail.
» Turn right onto a dirt footpath at the sign for the Gambel Oak Trail.
» Cross Paddington Drive and walk up Euston Drive.
» Turn right onto Paddington Drive.
» Turn left onto High Street.
» Turn left onto Paddington Drive again and find a footpath just before the road bends right. Take the footpath back to the Rail Trail.
» Turn left onto the Rail Trail and quickly turn right onto the Kearns Bike Path.
» Pass a storage area, come to a parking lot and find a sidewalk to your left between buildings.
» Turn left onto this sidewalk and continue on it, crossing Gold Dust Lane and Poison Creek Lane. Follow it through a plaza and around a bend to the start.

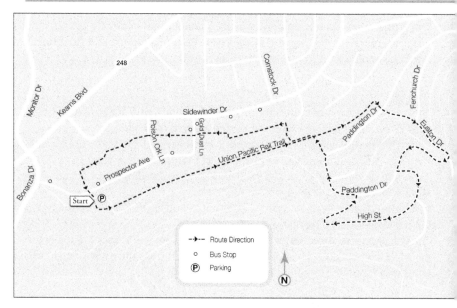

#13 Chatham Hills - Prospector Square

#14 Thaynes Canyon

Description: This route takes you through a neighborhood nestled at the base of the Park City Resort and meandering around the Muni golf course. Find picturesque ranches, residences, and ski terrain access.

Distance: 2.4 miles (3.8 kg)
Elevation Gain: 200 feet (61 m)
Peak Elevation: 6,918 feet (2,128 m)
Difficulty: INTERMEDIATE. There are a few short, moderately steep inclines and a long gentle incline at the end.
Surface: Pavement, and a few steps on dirt footpaths.

The Park City Muni is a wonderfully walkable and scenic public golf course.

Cautions: Minimal vehicular and cyclist traffic and maybe errant golf balls.
Restrooms are available at the Park City and Silver Star Resorts and the Hotel Park City golf/ski clubhouse.

Notable Features:

- **Glenwood Cemetery** was established in 1885 and is still in use. Avoid contact with the fragile grave markers.

- **Silver Star Plaza** is a ski-in-out resort featuring lodging, dining, shopping, rental equipment, concerts, **trail** access and tours. Note the Spiro Tunnel as you exit the plaza. Before chairlifts, skiers rode a mine train through this tunnel to a hoist, to be lifted up the mountain.

- Park City Municipal **Golf Course** becomes the White Pine **Cross-Country** skiing course in winter, with groomed trails for classic and skate skiing. Ponds on 11 holes make the course an oasis for wildlife.

Glenwood Cemetery tells of the struggles of Park City's early settlers. Photo by Ken Hurwitz MD

- The amenities of **Park City Resort**, as described in walks #2 and #3 are also accessible from this route.

Directions:

* Take the **bus** to Park City Resort and turn right out of the bus. Walk north to, or **park** in the NW corner of the north parking lot where there's a short footpath down to a sidewalk along condominiums, just north of the chairlifts. Descend on the footpath and follow the sidewalk to the road. You'll see the Glenwood Cemetery on the left. Find a walker's entrance right of the cemetery gate.
* If you've skipped or exited from the cemetery, follow Silver King Drive east to a left turn, Three Kings Drive.
* Turn left on Three Kings and proceed north to Crescent Ridge Road.
* Turn left onto Crescent Ridge and ascend until you see a pedestrian path forking right, as the road bends left.
* Turn right on this path and proceed towards the chair lift. Exit the plaza to the north, past the parking and down to Three Kings Drive.
* Turn left onto Three Kings and proceed to a four-way intersection.
* Turn right onto Thaynes Canyon Drive. Beware of the golf course driving range on the right. After passing Hotel Park City, find a paved path bordering the west side of Route 224.
* Turn right onto this path and proceed until it ends at Silver King Drive.
* Cross Silver King to another sidewalk and turn right to return to the resort's northern **parking** lot or the **bus** stop.

Route Summary:

» Start in the NW corner of the north parking area of Park City Resort.
» Take the dirt footpath to the sidewalk north of the chairlifts.
» Follow the sidewalk to a road and Glenwood Cemetery. Upon exiting the cemetery, follow Silver King Drive east to Three Kings Drive.
» Turn left onto Three Kings and proceed to Crescent Ridge Road and turn left.
» Ascend Crescent Ridge and turn right on a path as the road bends left.
» Proceed through the Silver Star Plaza back to Three Kings Drive.
» Turn left onto Three Kings and proceed to a 4-way intersection.
» Turn right onto Thaynes Canyon Drive and proceed to the end.
» Turn right onto a path along 224, and continue on it until it ends.
» Cross Silver King Drive and turn right to return to the bus stop or parking area at Park City Resort.

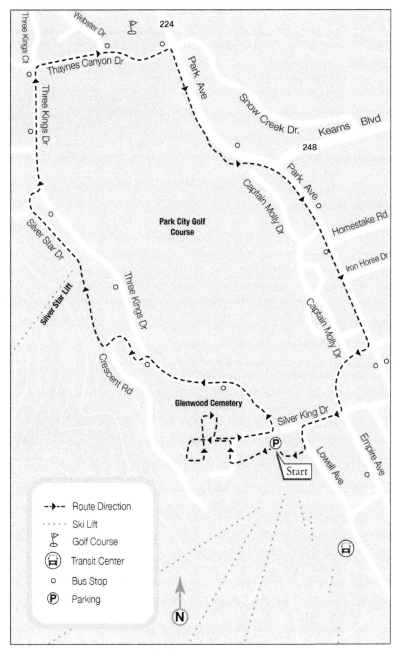

#14 Thaynes Canyon

#15 Farm Trail - McLeod Creek Trail

Description: The paved trails of this route will take you along Park City's entry corridor and through the property of the iconic McPolin barn. The trails follow streams and provide benches for taking in the views.

The McPolin barn was constructed from recycled timbers in 1908, without the use of nails.
Photo by Ken Hurwitz MD

Distance: 3.5 miles (5.6 km)
Elevation Gain: 148 feet (45 m)
Peak Elevation: 6,825 feet (2,080 m)
Difficulty: INTERMEDIATE due to a gentle but long ascent for the first half of this loop.
Surface: All paved paths and roads.
Cautions: Some road crossings and people traffic. The Farm Trail is inaccessible to walkers during ski season. There may also be skiers on the groomed McLeod Creek Trail.
Restrooms are available in the back of the building NW of the McPolin barn, the Hotel Park City golf/ski clubhouse, and at some Snow Creek plaza businesses.

Notable Features:

- The iconic McPolin white barn attracts photographers and painters from around the world. **Daniel McPolin** bought the 80-acre farm in 1897 for $600.00 to help feed early settlers. Veterinarian Dr. D.A. Osguthorpe acquired the farm in 1947. When Route 224 became four lanes in 1990, and too busy for a cattle crossing, Dr. Osguthorpe sold the property to Park City Municipal for preserved **open space.** The barn serves as a community facility. Vintage farm equipment is displayed along paths around the buildings.

There were human, animal and steam powered ploughs before the gasoline-powered tractor was invented in 1892.
Photo by Ken Hurwitz MD

- Note the sandstone rock **quarry** when you exit the farm property to the west. In autumn, the **Farm Trail** hosts a scarecrow contest.
- A metal ring sculpture at a trailhead along the Farm Trail captures views of the 2002 **Olympic** ski slopes.
- Richards Ranch, south of the white barn, provides more than 18-acres of protected open space. Horses in summer pastures sometimes greet walkers.

Protected open space has historically been supported by federal laws that provide tax credit for landowners who donate their property or sell it at an affordable price to a land trust for community benefit. Landowners can also acquire conservation easements by retaining their land in an undeveloped state. The **Summit Land Conservancy**, private citizens, and voters have helped preserve public access to precious Park City property, as seen in this walk. At wesaveland. org, the Summit Land Conservancy provides information about protected lands in and around Park City.

⌇ The paved trail along McLeod Creek, is ideal for **birding** and seeing **beaver** activity. Beavers build dams to create ponds around their lodges, constructed from trees, shrubs, rocks, mud, and castoreum, a unique glandular product secreted by beaver butts. A beaver lodge has a predator-safe underwater entrance, a foyer to dry off in, and a room on top for the beaver family to sleep and play in. It's unlikely you'll see the beavers though. They only work the night shift. Beaver habitat significantly improves water quality.

⌇ You might observe extreme athletes tumbling through the air in the **jump bike park** along the McLeod Creek Trail.

⌇ Snow Creek plaza provides shopping and dining options.

Directions:

∗ Take the bus to one of the farm **bus** stops on the east or west side of Route 224, or **park** at the trailhead on the east side of 224, opposite the white barn.

∗ Turn north out of the parking area and follow the paved path to a signpost, or turn south from the eastside bus stop and proceed to the signpost where an underpass takes you to the west side of Route 224.

∗ Turn right coming out of the tunnel and then turn left onto either of two paved paths into the farm property.

∗ Follow the paths around the buildings where plaques provide additional information, and arrive at another path at the farm's west end, the Farm Trail.

∗ Turn left heading south on this trail. It crosses Meadows Drive, Payday Drive, and Prospector Drive. The next corner is a four-way intersection at Thaynes Canyon Drive. Use the crosswalk pushbutton to carefully cross Route 224.

∗ Once across the highway, find a sidewalk alongside Snow Creek Drive. It crosses roads and bends into the Snow Creek shopping plaza and turns left. Find another paved path on the left, opposite the SW corner of the parking lot.

∗ Turn left onto this path, the McLeod Creek Trail. The path turns right and then left after crossing Saddle View Way. There are two more road crossings before the path returns to **parking** on the east side of Route 224. Find **bus** stops along Route 224 at Meadows Drive and across from the farm.

Route Summary:

» Take the bus to one of the stops near the white barn or park at the Farm Trailhead on the east side of Route 224.

» Cross under 224 through the tunnel and turn right and then left onto one of two paved paths into the farm.

» Find a blacktop path behind the farm and turn left onto it.

» Stay on the Farm Trail heading south and crossing Meadows, Payday and Prospector Drives. Continue to the four-way intersection at the corner of Thaynes Canyon Drive.

» Use the traffic control button to cross Route 224. On the east side find a sidewalk along Snow Creek Drive. Find a paved path to the left, at the SW corner of the shopping plaza.

» Turn left onto this path and follow it through some turns and street crossings back to the Farm Trailhead and bus stops.

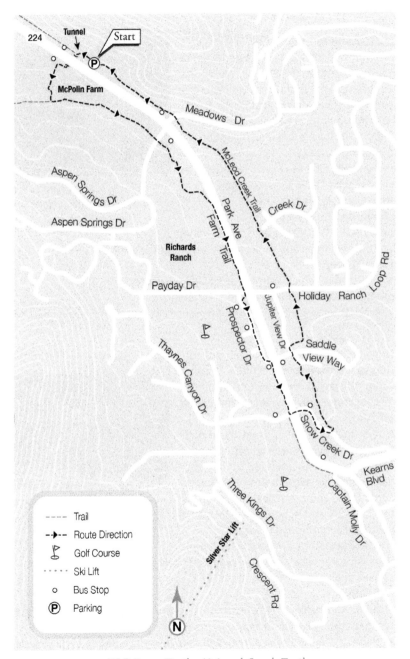

#15 Farm Trail - McLeod Creek Trail

#16 Aspen Springs

Description: This route, just west of Park City's entry corridor, winds through a serene alpine neighborhood set amidst aspens, spring fed water features, and luscious landscapes. It is approachable from several access points and provides maximal exercise for a quick, quiet walk. Bus riders have a less lengthy option.

Spring in Aspen Springs at sunset is a sublime time to walk.
Photo by Ken Hurwitz MD

Distance: about 2.5 miles (4 km) for drivers or 1.8 miles (2.9 km) from the bus stop.
Elevation Gain: 285 feet (87 m)
Peak Elevation: 7,035 feet (21 m)
Difficulty: INTERMEDIATE due to a long uphill climb at the beginning and a long gentle ascent at the end.
Surface: All paved.
Cautions: Possible vehicular traffic or wildlife encounters.
Restrooms are occasionally available at Rotary Park.

Notable Features:

- Enjoy unique **views** of the iconic McPolin Farm.
- **Horses** graze summer pastures. Walking when foliage is not in full array affords glimpses of magnificent mountain estates.
- A rock **quarry** projects from the mountainside above the highest perched homes. Lonely outcroppings of rocks signal tectonically active areas to geologists and miners, and can reveal the nature of the bedrock and sedimentary rock that was deposited through the ages.

Springs and ponds are created when gravity or pressure causes water in aquifers to flow to Earth's surface.

- A metal sculpture symbolic of **Olympic** rings captures views of ski terrain. Deer Valley Resort hosted Olympic slalom, aerials, and moguls events. Park City Resort hosted half-pipe and giant slalom competition.
- Richards Ranch, just north of Payday Drive, provides 18-acres of protected open space, as described in walk #15.
- At the west end of Payday Drive, where miners once picked up paychecks, find **Rotary Park**, a municipal facility that citizens can rent for private parties.

For butt-busting exercise, eye-popping architecture, and access to the tough **Iron Mountain Trail**, take a detour up Iron Canyon Drive instead of turning right on Delta Drive. Then turn right onto Iron Mountain Drive, loop back to Iron Canyon Drive, and turn left at the 4-way intersection onto Delta Drive to walk the loop as described below.

Directions:

* Find a **bus** stop on the west side of Route 224 at the south corner of Meadows Drive. From the bus stop, proceed west on Meadows Drive, turn left onto Aspen Springs Drive, loop back to Meadows Drive, and turn left to return to the bus stop.
* **Drivers** should turn west off of Route 224 onto Payday Drive and proceed to Rotary Park and limited parking at the end of the street. Walk east on Payday, and immediately turn left onto Iron Canyon Drive. Continue uphill to an intersection with Delta Drive.
* Turn right onto Delta, a short street.
* From Delta Drive turn left onto Aspen Springs Drive, and follow it up, around and down a big horseshoe, ignoring two left turns.
* After passing a ranch behind the white barn, turn left onto Meadows Drive and follow it to Route 224.
* Find a **bus** stop on the SW corner of the intersection of Meadows Drive and Route 224. **Drivers** should turn right onto a paved trail just before the highway, the Farm Trail. If you're tired, consider a bus ride from here to the next stop, just past Payday Drive. The rest of this walk is up a gentle grade. If still walking, follow the paved path past the Olympic Rings trailhead to the intersection at Payday Drive.
* Turn right onto Payday. Your vehicle is at the end of this street.

Route Summary:

» Bus riders ascend Meadows Drive. Turn left onto Aspens Springs Drive and follow it around and back to Meadows Drive for the bus.
» Drivers should walk east from Rotary Park at the west end of Payday Drive and turn left onto Iron Canyon Drive.
» Turn right onto Delta Drive.
» Turn left onto Aspen Springs Drive and follow it to a 3rd left turn, Meadows Drive.
» Turn left onto Meadows Drive and follow it to a paved path just before Route 224.
» Turn right onto the paved path, the Farm Trail and follow it south, back to the corner of Payday Drive.
» Turn right on Payday and return to the end of the street.

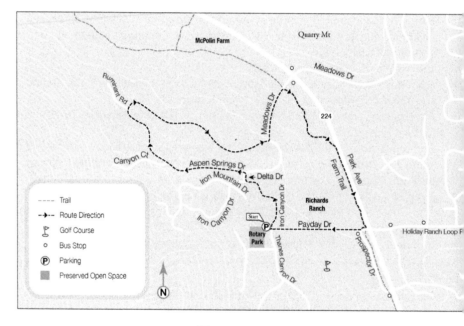

#16 Aspen Springs

#17 Park Meadows

Description: This suburban neighborhood, once occupied by ranches, now provides residents and school kids with spectacular views of the mountains and the water features of the Park Meadows Golf Course.

Fairways and ponds embellish the mountain views of Park Meadows. Photo by Ken Hurwitz MD

Distance: 4.9 miles (7.9 km)
Elevation Gain: 131 feet (40 m)
Peak Elevation: 6,693 feet (2040 m)
Difficulty: INTERMEDIATE due to its length. Inclines are gentle but there's a mild ascent at the end.
Surface: All paved.
Cautions: Vehicular and cyclist traffic.
Restrooms are available in Creekside Park. Another option is a detour to the MARC or school ball field facility as described in Walk #11.

Notable Features:

- Creekside Park provides parking, **playgrounds** with agility features, and a jump bike park.
- Many golf greats played the Jack Nicklaus course of the Park Meadows Country Club, formerly a venue for the Senior Major Championships.
- Park Meadows provides **trail connections** to Quarry Mountain, PC Hill, Round Valley and McLeod Creek. And, when it's getting dark and chilly on Park City's west side, Park Meadows is still sunny and warm.
- The Municipal Athletic and Recreation Center (the **MARC**) offers gyms, pools, courts, and classes for residents and visitors.

Bouncing off bumps on dirt bikes is just one more way Park City athletes get airborne. Photo by Ken Hurwitz MD

Directions:

- Start at the **bus** stop on Holiday Ranch Loop Road across the street from Creekside Park. **Drivers** turn east off of Rt. 224 onto Holiday Ranch Loop. Proceed a short way to a 2nd right turn into Creekside Park where there's limited parking.
- Exiting Creekside Park, turn right onto a paved path along Holiday Ranch Loop Road. Follow to an intersection with Little Kate Road.

* Turn right onto Little Kate and proceed a short way to an intersection with Lucky John Drive. (If you briefly continue straight on Little Kate, you can detour to the MARC.)
* Turn right onto Lucky John and follow it around a bend and past schoolyards. Lucky John becomes Meadows Drive. Continue on Meadows to an intersection with Fairway Village Drive.
* Turn left onto Fairway Village and proceed uphill to the intersection with Sunny Slopes Drive.
* Turn left onto Sunny Slopes and proceed downhill to a gate with pedestrian bypasses on each side. After the gate, the road bends right and goes uphill back to Meadows Drive.
* Turn left onto Meadows, and quickly turn left onto American Saddler Drive. Proceed to a T-intersection with Lucky John Drive.
* Turn left onto Lucky John and proceed to Little Kate Road.
* Turn right onto Little Kate and proceed to the intersection with Holiday Ranch Loop Road.
* Turn left onto Holiday Ranch and follow the pedestrian path on the east side of the road back to the **bus** stop and **parking**.

Route Summary:

» Start at Creekside Park on Holiday Ranch Loop Road.
» Exit the park and turn right onto Holiday Ranch.
» Turn right onto Little Kate Road.
» Turn right onto Lucky John Drive. It becomes Meadows Drive.
» Turn left onto Fairway Village Drive.
» Turn left onto Sunny Slopes Drive. Follow it around a bend and through either side of a gate and back to Meadows Drive.
» Turn left onto Meadows.
» Turn left onto American Saddler Drive.
» Turn left onto Lucky John Drive.
» Turn right onto Little Kate Road.
» Turn left, back onto Holiday Ranch Loop Road to return to start.

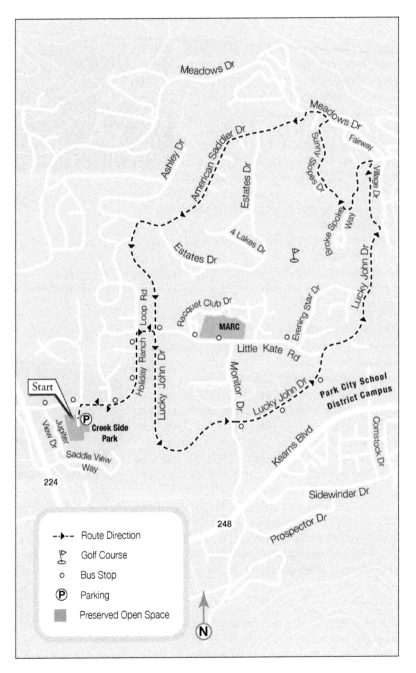

Legend

- --▸-- Route Direction
- ⚑ Golf Course
- ○ Bus Stop
- Ⓟ Parking
- ▓ Preserved Open Space

#17 Park Meadows

#18 PC Hill

Description: This walk is about a good climb on great trails with outstanding views, especially for looking down on football games and the annual Autumn Aloft Balloon Festival.

Hot air balloon rides are a favorite Park City adventure. Photo by Jon Scarlet

Distance: 3.24 miles (5.2 km)
Elevation Gain: 536 feet (163 m)
Peak Elevation: 7,170 feet (2,185 m)
Difficulty: DIFFICULT due to a long steep climb to start.
Surface: Some pavement, mostly single-track with small rocks and roots.
Cautions: Possible crowds for special events. Following directions should enable you to avoid fooler trails.
Restrooms are available if you detour to the ball fields as in Walk #11.

Notable Features:

- The big white letters "PC", painted across the mountain's west face overlooking the "North Forty" football field, represent Park City school spirit. The custom of imprinting hillsides, (**mountain monograms**), has fueled passionate opponents and supporters. When a big "U" was crumbling on a hillside above the University of Utah in 2006, "letter lovers" donated more than $200,000.00 for repairs.
- On top of PC Hill, there's a dedication rock engraved with the names of contributors to Park City's protected open space and trails.
- The return loop of this walk provides some summer shade, connects to the Round Valley **trail** system, and traverses a neighborhood of mountain mansions.
- Enjoy connecting **trails** into **wetlands** within the school campus and don't miss the bird song coming from the "sanctuary" at the south end of the athletic field.

Controversial mountain monograms are seen mostly in the western USA.

Directions:

* Take the **bus** to the stop at the corner of Kearns Boulevard and Comstock Avenue. Then walk east along the north side of Kearns Boulevard. Walkers and **drivers** should turn north off of Route 248, Kearns Boulevard, just east of the school campus buildings and just west of PC Hill. Follow this narrow road to a

trailhead parking area.

* Find the PC Hill Trail opposite a footbridge. Turn right onto this trail to begin the climb, and ascend through a switchback.
* When you come to a fork, bear right, switching back again. Continue the climb going south. Ignore two fooler trails to the left and one to the right.
* At the next fork, bear left. The trail bends east. Stay on the path that appears most used, avoiding more fooler trails.
* Notice a left turn as a fence comes into view ahead. There's a trail to the left before the fence, and another trail along the fence. Turn left onto either trail and proceed through the next left turn onto a trail that bends west and takes you to the "PC" letters.
* From the letters, take the trail after either the big "P" or "C". Both trails go a short distance to the mountaintop where there are more trails, including "PC Hill Trail" to the east.
* Take the PC Hill Trail, following it through switchbacks as it descends the mountain. Cross a double-track road and stay on the single-track until you come to a fork with a sign for the Quinn Recreation Trail.
* Bear left at this fork and quickly arrive at the Hat Trick Trail.
* Turn left onto Hat Trick and continue to the next intersection with the Fairway Hills Connector Trail.
* Turn left onto Fairway Hills Connector and the trail will end in the cul-de-sac of Morning Sky Court. Continue downhill on Morning Sky to its end on Silver Cloud Drive.
* Turn left onto Silver Cloud and follow it downhill to Meadows Drive.
* Turn left onto Meadows Drive and cautiously walk in the bike lane. Just past a private drive on the left, (that looks like a road), find a blacktop path that goes back to the school fields, and a sign pointing to the Rail Trail.
* Turn left onto this path and bear right onto a woodchip trail bordering a fence that goes around the school field. This trail takes you past the "sanctuary" on the south end of the field. On the east side of the field find a footbridge over a creek crossing back to the **parking** at the base of PC Hill. From the trailhead, exit south to Kearns Boulevard. To get to the **bus,** turn right onto Kearns Boulevard and walk west.

Route Summary:

» Start at the PC Trailhead at the east end of the school campus and west of PC Hill.
» Turn right onto the PC Hill Trail and begin the climb.
» Proceed through two switchbacks, bearing right at an intersection. Ignore two "fooler" trails to the left and one to the right. You will come to a fork.
» Bear left. Stay on the trail that appears most used.
» Notice two left turns as a fence comes into view. Take either and proceed as these trails turn left and bend west to arrive at the "PC".

» Take either of the trails that start above the big "P" or "C", to the top of the mountain.

» Take the PC Hill Trail on the east side of the mountaintop. At an intersection with double-track, cross the road to stay on the single-track. Arrive at a fork with a sign to the Quinn Recreation Trail.

» Bear left at this fork and quickly arrive at the Hat Trick Trail.

» Turn left onto the Hat Trick Trail.

» Turn left onto Fairway Hills Connector Trail, and proceed to Morning Sky Court. Walk downhill to Silver Cloud Drive.

» Turn left on Silver Cloud.

» Turn left onto Meadows Drive and continue past a private drive to a blacktop path on the left.

» Turn left onto this blacktop.

» Bear right onto a woodchip path encircling the athletic field to arrive at a footbridge that returns to the parking area at the base of PC Hill.

» Bus riders should turn right onto Kearns Boulevard to return to the bus stop.

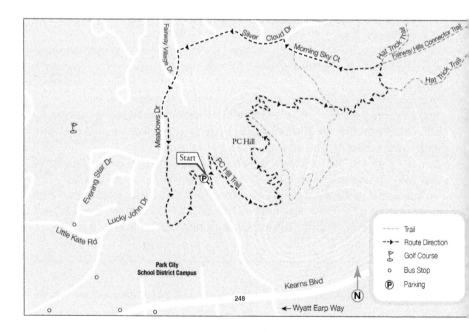

#18 PC Hill

#19 The Cove - Quarry Mountain

Description: This short off-road walk above the Park Meadows neighborhood takes you through surprisingly diverse landscapes on well-maintained trails.

Trailhead bulletin boards provide important information for savvy trail users.

Distance: 1.3 miles (2.0 km)
Elevation Gain: 125 feet (38 m)
Peak Elevation: 6,931 feet (1,871 m)
Difficulty: INTERMEDIATE due to a mild but steady climb at the start.
Surface: Dirt paths and sidewalk and some slightly rocky terrain.
Cautions: Possible cyclist, skier or equestrian traffic. Follow directions; intersecting trails lead to private property.
Restrooms are not available, but mitt-mitts may be.

Notable Features:

❧ In 2014, Park City Municipal procured 53 acres of protected open space on Risner Ridge, at the foot of Quarry Mountain. In addition to its role as a **view shed** this terrain supports elk, moose, mule deer, red foxes, rabbits, squirrels, hawks, eagles, and other **wildlife,** as well as walkers, equestrians and snowshoers.

❧ Some of this route feels like remote country. You will briefly traverse a rock **quarry**.

❧ This route can easily be **combined** with Walk #20, Lah Dee Duh. They share a starting point but offer different vistas.

Directions:

✳ Unless bus service expands to the NE corner of Park Meadows, expect a 1¼-mile (2 km) uphill walk to the trailhead from the **bus** stop on Little Kate Road and Evening Star Drive. From the bus stop (shown on Map #21), proceed east on Little Kate to an intersection.

✳ Turn left onto Lucky John Drive. It turns into Meadows Drive. After a second climb and a big bend left, find a trailhead on the right.

✳ **Drivers** turn east off of Route 224 at its intersection with Meadows Drive. Proceed up a long hill and look for a trailhead with parking on the left

Risner Ridge serves as a wildlife refuge.

before the road bends south. (Bus riders could take the drivers' route but a long steep climb requires a high level of fitness.)

* Find a dirt trail, the Rossman Trail, across the street from the Cove Trailhead Bear right onto this trail. Ignore turnoffs and arrive at a road.
* Cross the road to pick up the trail on the opposite side. It winds around a flat boulder and quickly intersects with gravel double-track.
* Turn right onto this double-track and proceed uphill. Follow the road as it bends left around a water tank, and then downhill to a T-intersection with single-track.
* Turn left onto the single-track. Follow this trail to arrive at another T-intersection. (To take a short detour to a lookout, turn right at the T to arrive at a bench dedicated to the trail's namesake, Norman Rossman, a New York City builder who adored Park City.)
* To skip the lookout, turn left at the T-intersection and it becomes a double-track (Returning from the lookout, bear right at this intersection.) Proceed to a four-way intersection.
* Turn left onto a gravel road and follow it to Meadows Drive.
* **Drivers** should turn left onto Meadows and proceed back to the trailhead. **Bus** riders can turn right onto Meadows and follow it to the bus stop at its intersection with Route 224, a long walk, but mostly downhill. Or, retrace your route to the starting bus stop on Little Kate Road and Evening Star.

Route Summary:

» Start at the Cove Trailhead along Meadows Drive in the NE corner of the Park Meadows neighborhood.
» Cross the street from the trailhead and turn right onto the Rossman Trail. Follow it to a paved road.
» Cross the road and pick up the same trail between some rocks. Proceed a short way to an intersection.
» Turn right and ascend on a dirt road to the left side of a water tank. Follow the road downhill to an intersection with a single-track.
» Turn left and proceed to the next trail intersection.
» Turn left and proceed to another intersection.
» Turn left onto a gravel road and follow it to Meadows Drive.
» Turn left onto the sidewalk along Meadows to return to parking at the Cove Trailhead. Bus riders can turn right onto Meadows and walk downhill to a bus stop at the intersection with Route 224, or turn left to return to start.

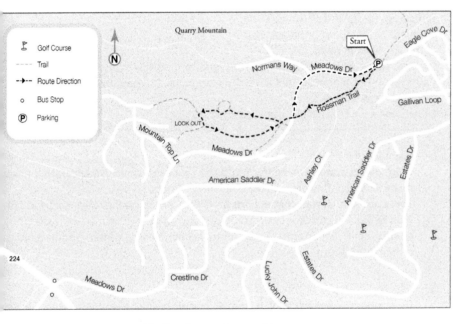

#19 The Cove - Quarry Mountain

#20 Lah Dee Duh

Description: On the east edge of suburban Park City, walkers will find a network of well-maintained trails traversing the preserved open space of Round Valley. The Cove Trailhead is one of several access points to this expansive system.

The Lah Dee Duh Trail offers great views of the Snyderville Basin. Photo by Nick Calas

Distance: 1.3 miles (2.0 km)
Elevation Gain: 92 feet (28 m)
Peak Elevation: 6,875 feet (2,096 m)
Difficulty: INTERMEDIATE due to moderately steep but short inclines at the start and midway.
Surface: Single-track, mostly smooth dirt, and some mildly rocky terrain.
Cautions: This is a popular trail for cyclists, dog walkers, snowshoers, skiers, and occasionally equestrians.
Restrooms are not available, but mutt mitts may be.

Notable Features:

- **Wildflowers** abound along this trail. Look for onion, chicory, paintbrush, prickly pears, lilies, sunflowers, and many other bloomers.
- There are several **trail connections** here. Find a map on the Cove Trailhead bulletin board. This route is easily combined with Walk #19 with which it shares its starting point. For information about trail conditions, or **winter grooming**, go to mountaintrails.org.

Directions:

* Unless **bus** service expands to the NE corner of Park Meadows, expect a 1¼-mile (2 km) uphill walk to the trailhead from the bus stop on Little Kate Road at Evening Star Drive. From the bus stop (see map #21) proceed east on Little Kate to Lucky John Drive and turn left.
* Lucky John Drive turns into Meadows Drive. After a second climb and big bend to the left, find a trailhead on the right.
* **Drivers** can get to the trailhead by turning east off of Route 224 at the intersection of Meadows Drive. Proceed up a long hill and look for a trailhead with parking on the left before the road bends south.
* From the Cove Trailhead, follow the rocky dirt road uphill. Bear right at the first fork, left at the second, and left at the third fork onto a single-track, the Lah Dee

Duh Trail. Proceed until you notice an unmarked trail to the left, shortly before seeing a trail marker for Cammy's Trail on the right.

* Turn left onto this unmarked downhill single-track. Go about a tenth of a mile (0.17 km) and find another single-track trail to the right.
* Turn right and briefly climb rock steps for another tenth of a mile (0.17 km) to reconnect with Lah Dee Duh.
* Turn right onto Lah Dee Duh and follow it back to the trailhead and parking, taking right turns at intersections.
* From the trailhead, **bus** riders can bear left onto Meadows Drive and follow it to Evening Star Drive. Turn right on Evening Star and then right again onto Little Kate to the bus stop.
* **Bus** riders could also turn right onto Meadows Drive, as should **drivers**, and take the long route up and then mostly downhill to a bus stop at the intersection of Meadows with Route 224.

Route Summary:

» Start at the Cove Trailhead along Meadows Drive in the NE corner of the Park Meadows neighborhood.

» From the trailhead, head east uphill where you'll come to three forks. Bear right at the first, left at the second, and left at the third fork onto the Lah Dee Duh Trail.

» Follow this single-track to an unmarked trail on the left, just before a sign to Cammy's Trail. Turn left onto this unnamed single-track.

» Turn right onto the next unmarked single-track and briefly ascend back to Lah Dee Duh.

» Turn right and follow Lah Dee Duh back to the start, bearing right at intersections.

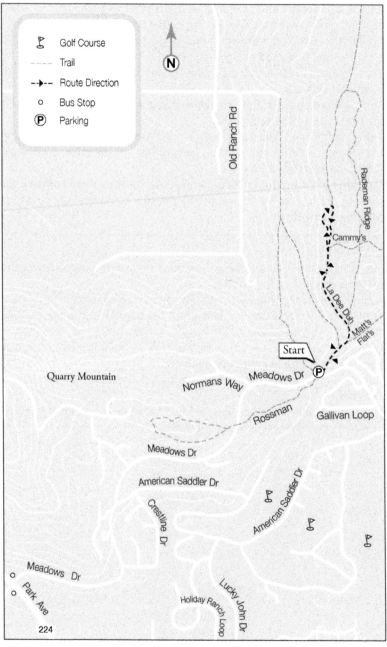

#20 Lah Dee Duh

#21 Fairway Hills

Description: A bounty of groomed trails traverses open space between the Park Meadows neighborhood and Quinn's Junction. This route takes you past lush farmland and some exquisite residences.

The soft, smooth trails of Round Valley are local favorites.

Distance: 1.8 miles (2.9 km)
Elevation Gain: 125 feet (38 m)
Peak Elevation: 6,930 feet (2,112 m)
Difficulty: EASY. The elevation gain is distributed widely.
Surface: Mostly roadbed on single and double-track. Some pavement.
Cautions: Minimal vehicular traffic but maybe many cyclists or skate skiers. Study the landscape before taking detours into the trail maze.
Restrooms are not available. Mutt-mitts might be.

Notable Features:

- This walk is an interesting blend of gentrified and native. Check the trailhead bulletin board regarding potential **wildlife** encounters.
- Find maps and more information about **trail connections** on the trailhead bulletin board and at mountaintrails.org.

Directions:

* Unless **bus** service expands to the NE corner of Park Meadows, expect a 1¼ (2 km) uphill walk to the trailhead from the bus stop on Little Kate Road at Evening Star Drive. From the bus stop, proceed east on Little Kate to Lucky John Drive and turn left.
* **Drivers** turn north off of Route 248 onto Monitor Drive and proceed to the first intersection with Lucky John Drive and turn right.
* Lucky John becomes Meadows Drive. Proceed on Meadows to Sunny Slopes Drive and turn right.
* Proceed uphill to the second left turn, Fairway Hills Court.
* Turn left onto Fairway Hills and immediately turn right onto Round Valley Way and proceed to parking and a trailhead in the cul-de-sac. Be careful of the bump entering the parking area.
* After checking the trailhead notices, proceed to the end of the parking.
* Turn right onto the Fast Pitch Trail and proceed on this single-track about a third of a mile (0.53 km) to the first right turn.

* Turn right onto the Hat Trick Trail and proceed about a half-mile (0.8 km) until you come to an intersecting trail, Fairway Hills Connector.
* Turn right onto the Connector and follow this trail until it ends on a cul-de-sac. Descend on the sidewalk to Silver Cloud Drive.
* Cross Silver Cloud. Find a double-track trail behind a fire hydrant. Follow this trail to Sunny Slopes Drive, ignoring forks along the way.
* Cross Sunny Slopes, turn left, and descend to a four-way intersection with Fairway Hills Court.
* If you came by **bus**, continue down Sunny Slopes to Meadows Drive. Turn left on Meadows and follow it to Evening Star. Turn right on Evening Star and follow it to the bus stop on Little Kate Road.
* **Drivers** should turn right onto Fairway Hills Court and immediately turn right again onto Round Valley Way.
* Exiting the parking area (with bump), turn left, then right, then left onto Meadows Drive, and follow it to Monitor Drive.
* Turn left onto Monitor to return to Rt. 248.

Route Summary:

» Start at the Round Valley Trailhead at the end of Round Valley Way, at the east end of Park Meadows.
» Pass the trailhead bulletin board and turn right onto the Fast Pitch trail at the end of the parking area.
» Proceed to the first trail intersection and turn right onto the Hat Trick Trail.
» Proceed to an intersection and turn right onto the Fairway Hills Connector Trail, which ends on Morning Sky Court.
» Descend the road to Silver Cloud Drive, cross the street and find a double-track gravelly trail behind a fire hydrant. Proceed on this trail until it ends on Sunny Slopes Drive.
» Cross Sunny Slopes to the sidewalk and turn left. Descend to a four-way intersection.
» Bus riders continue down Sunny Slopes and turn left onto Meadows to return to the bus stop.
» Motorists turn right onto Fairway Hills Court and make another quick right onto Round Valley Way to return to the trailhead parking area.

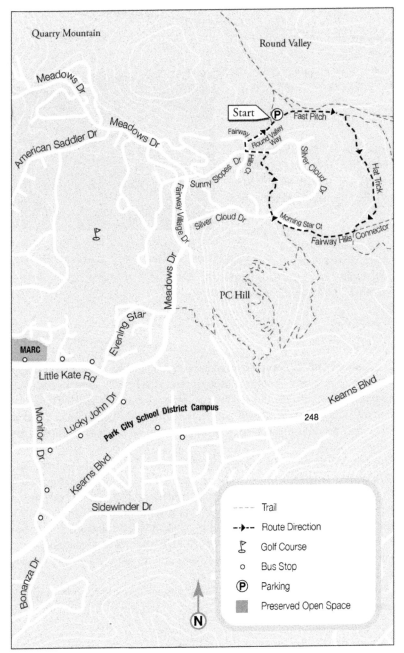

#21 Fairway Hills

#22 Quinn's Junction

Description: This easy off-road hike has been included to showcase the amenities of the Quinn's Junction Sports Complex and Round Valley.

Round Valley provides 690 acres of open space and 30 miles (48km) of trails, but barely 7% of Park City's vast trail system.

Distance: This is a one-mile (1.6 km) loop.
Elevation Gain: 62 feet (19 m)
Peak Elevation: 6,718 ft. (2,048 m)
Difficulty: EASY, though all off-road.
Surface: Red dirt roadbed with small rocks.
Cautions: This trail is very popular with many kinds of users.
Restrooms are available in the free-standing facility near the ball fields and parking. Mutt mitts may be available.

Notable Features:

~ The **Quinn's Sports Complex** provides ball fields, a playground and **dog parks**. Watch a championship softball tournament, or a hockey game or figure skating competition at the Park City Ice Arena after your walk. **Ice-skating** on a hot summer afternoon is a cool delight. Summer clothes will work if you just add gloves, but small children are closer to the ice and need warmer clothes, especially gloves.

~ This short walk will take you past lush farmland and facilities of the **National Ability Center (NAC)**, a non-profit established in 1985. Due to the presence of the NAC, you may encounter **adaptive athletes** skiing, golfing, cycling, and on horseback, or watch an exciting sled hockey game at the ice rink. The NAC has the mission to empower individuals of all abilities by building self-esteem, confidence and lifetime skills through sport, recreation, and educational programs. For more information about the NAC and how to get involved, go to www.discovernac.org.

~ Check the trailhead bulletin board or mountaintrails.org for information about **trails** and **winter** grooming.

Directions:

* Unless Park City Transit establishes regular bus service to Quinn's Junction, **bus** riders can arrange for free shared bus service by calling Dial-A-Ride at 435.640.7819.
* **Drivers** turn west off of Route 248 onto Round Valley Drive at the traffic light west of Route 40. Take the first left turn onto Gillmor Way. Park in the second parking area near the ball fields. Find the Quinn's Trailhead bulletin board across the road where three trails start. Take the middle trail, Fast Pitch, and proceed to an intersection.
* Turn right onto the Hat Trick Trail and follow it back to the trailhead.

Route Summary:

» Start at the Quinn's Junction Trailhead on Gilmore Way.
» From the trailhead bulletin board, take the middle trail.
» Turn right onto the Hat Trick Trail, which loops back to start.

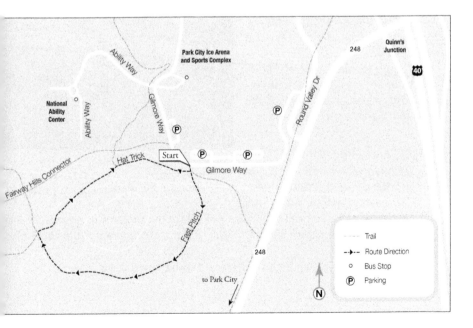

#22 Quinn's Junction

#23 Willow Creek Park

Description: Multiple walking routes and amenities are available in this 17.5-acre community park adjoined by 66 acres of open space.

Distance, Surface and **Difficulty** for three walks: These are all EASY short walks on level trails that may be groomed in winter.

- The shortest of the walks is 0.33 miles (0.5 km) and is all blacktop.
- A one-mile (1.6 km) loop around the Willow Creek and Split Rail Trails includes level blacktop and roadbed.
- A longer loop of 1.83 miles (2.9 km) from Willow Creek to the East Connector Trail includes blacktop, roadbed and wooden bridges.

Elevation Gain: 70 feet (21 m) is the maximum.

Peak Elevation: 6,558 feet (2,008 m)

Cautions: Possibly fast moving or inexperienced cyclists and skiers.

Restrooms are available near the parking area.

Notable Features:

- An off-leash **dog park** provides paths, shade, **agility features**, and a **dog pond** with a floating dock.
- There's **ice-skating** on the pond in winter, conditions permitting.
- Find playgrounds, sports fields and courts, and picnic facilities.

Equipment with instructions at 10 exercise stations can turn your workout into a walk in the park, or your walk into a workout.

Directions (Route Summary):

- **Drivers** should take Route 224 to Old Ranch Road and turn east. The nearest **bus** stop is on the NE corner of Rt. 224 and Old Ranch Road. Take the sidewalk or drive along Old Ranch, which bends left and then right. Find the park on your left in about 0.65 miles (1.05 km).
- **Maps** and **signs** within the park provide directions and options.

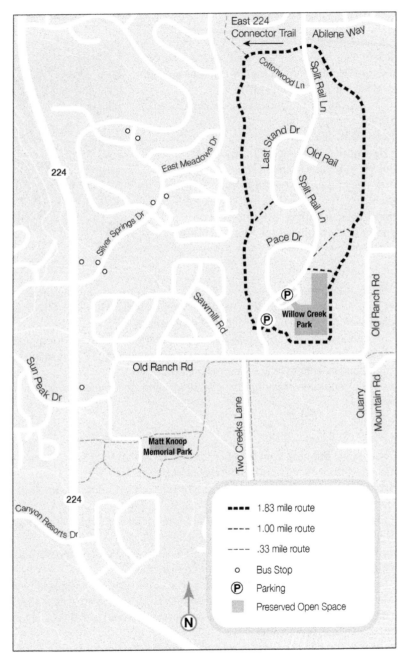

#23 Willow Creek Park

#24 Matt Knoop Park - McLeod Creek Trail

Description: This may be the most surprising and rewarding of easy walks. See the front cover of this book to view the McLeod Creek Trail in summer splendor. (Cover photo by Ken Hurwitz MD)

Distance: 2.5 miles (4 km)
Elevation Gain: 161 feet (49 m)
Peak Elevation: 6,728 feet (2,051 m)
Difficulty: EASY, fairly level terrain.
Surface: Paved paths, wooden bridges and some dirt footpath.
Cautions: Popular with cyclists and skiers.
Restrooms are available at the Matt Knoop Park.

Amusing art is an added feature of this scenic route.

Notable Features:

- The Matt Knoop Memorial Park honors a local graduate and soccer star killed in a hit-and-run accident. This 10-acre community park has a turf field, shaded playground, picnic pavilions, and **trail** connections.
- This route passes the **Copper Moose Organic Farm**, which seeks to connect people with the agriculture of their bioregion. To see when the farm stand is open to the public, check www.coppermoosefarm.com.
- Consult mountaintrails.org for conditions and grooming status for **winter** walking.

Directions:

- The nearest **bus** stop is on the NE corner of Rt. 224 and Old Ranch Road. **Drivers** turn east from Rt. 224 onto Old Ranch Road.
- From Old Ranch Road, take the first right turn onto Shadow Mountain Drive. It bends into parking areas.
- From the parking, take Miss Billy's Trail south of the turf field, walking east. This trail bends left and comes to an intersecting trail.
- Turn right and the trail quickly bends left again. It will bend right before paralleling Old Ranch Road and crossing Two Creeks Lane.
- Quickly turn right onto roadbed after crossing Two Creeks, and continue on the McLeod Creek Trail as it makes two 90-degree turns and crosses a boardwalk. Look for sculpted metal flowers. Pass between them and follow a footpath through a wooded area to a fork.
- Bear left at the fork and follow the path around Temple Har Shalom.
- Make a left onto a road into the temple parking lot and follow it west to Route

224. Find a pedestrian path alongside the highway.

* Turn right heading north on this path and proceed past two intersections until you come to a gravel road on the right, marked Miss Billy's Bypass and Ike's Pump Track. **Bus** riders should stay on the pedestrian path along Route 224 to the Old Ranch Road bus stop.

* **Drivers** should turn right off the pedestrian path towards Miss Billy's, and follow the path, bearing right at the fork, until arriving back at the parking in Matt Knoop Park.

Route Summary:

» Start at the parking lots of Matt Knoop Memorial Park.

» Take Miss Billy's Trail on the south side of the turf field. It bends left before arriving at an intersection.

» Turn right at the intersection and follow this trail through bends and a road intersection, Two Creeks Lane.

» After crossing Two Creeks, immediately turn right onto roadbed. Follow it through turns and over a wooden bridge.

» Take the footpath between metal flowers through woods to a fork.

» Bear left and proceed around Temple Har Shalom and parking. Continue out the entrance road to Route 224.

» Turn right onto a paved path alongside the highway. Walk north past two intersections and come to Miss Billy's Bypass Trail on your right.

» Bus riders should stay on the path along Route 224 to the bus stop at the corner of Old Ranch Road.

» Drivers should turn right onto Miss Billy's and walk back to the parking areas at Matt Knoop Park.

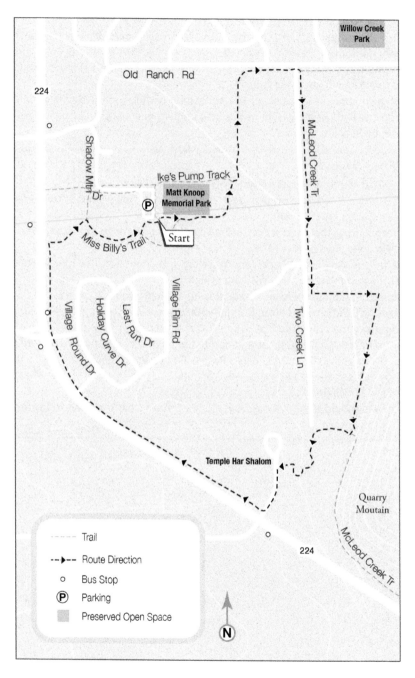

#24 Matt Knoop Park - McLeod Creek Trail

#25 Swaner Preserve - Redstone

Description: This short easy walk takes you on a neighborhood trail around the periphery of a nature preserve.

Distance: 1.5 miles (2.4 km)
Elevation: 33 feet (10 m)
Peak Elevation: 6,428 feet (1,959 m)
Difficulty: EASY, relatively level.
Surface: Paved trails and sidewalks.
Cautions: Some vehicular, cyclist and people traffic.
Restrooms may be found at various businesses in the commercial area.

Find a bobsled, obelisk, band shell, and plaza art at the Newpark Town Center.

Notable Features:

- **Swaner Memorial Park** ("The Preserve") was created by the Swaner Family in 1995 along with the land trust, Utah Open Lands. Conservation easements here support wildlife and protect 1,200 acres of open space and 800 acres of wetlands. There are 10 miles (16 km) of trails and a historic farm within the preserve.
- The Swaner Ecocenter, 1258 Center Drive, is an **ecology museum** with changing exhibits. Take a self-guided tour up an observation tower. **Guided tours** and **geocaching adventures** (treasure hunts using GPS devices) are also available. Depending on conditions, Ecocenter personnel can grant access to additional trails. **Snowshoe rentals** are available at the Ecocenter front desk in winter.
- The **obelisk** in the Newpark Town Center casts a shadow on the pavement showing the sun's motion through the calendar year.
- Dining and shopping opportunities are plentiful along this route and Jupiter Bowl provides another recreational option.

Directions:

* East of Rt. 224 at Kimball Junction, find a plaza east of Newpark Boulevard, with nearby bus stops on Newpark and Highland Drives and parking around the plaza. The Ecocenter is in the NE corner of the plaza. A paved path starts at the SW corner of the Ecocenter. Bear left from the plaza onto this path as it encircles townhomes.
* Bear right when the path intersects with the trail bordering Rt. 224.
* At the next trail intersection; turn right onto Redstone Center Drive, crossing under the arched sign. Proceed to a road intersection.
* Cross Highland Drive at the intersection and continue onto Center Drive, veering left back to the plaza, bus stops and parking.

Route Summary:

» Take the paved perimeter path from the SW corner of the Swaner Ecocenter around townhomes. Bear right when this path merges with a trail along Rt. 224.

» Turn right off of the trail along the highway onto store-lined Redstone Center Drive.

» Continue along this street when it crosses Highland Drive, veers left onto Center Drive, and ends back at the Ecocenter plaza.

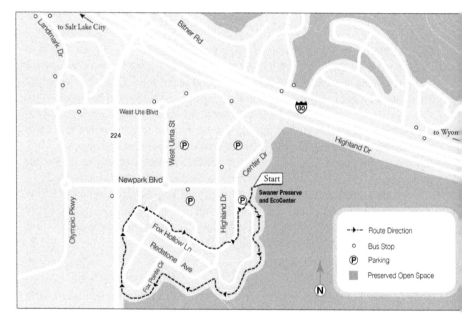

#25 Swaner Preserve - Redstone

#26 Over and Under Kimball Junction

Description: While some family members are shopping the outlets, this walk will entertain those in your group who would rather spend their leisure time outdoors. After dropping off the shoppers, walk out of the mall and enjoy this pedestrian route up, over, and down under roads and retail.

Another comical moose welcomes shoppers and walkers.

Distance: 2.8 miles (4.5 km)
Elevation Gain: 148 feet (45m)
Peak Elevation: 6,496 feet (1980 m)
Difficulty: EASY, though with some gentle inclines.
Surface: Sidewalk, blacktop and a few steps on a dirt footpath.
Cautions: Some road crossings with vehicular and possible cyclist traffic.
Restrooms are available at the mall, Visitor's Center, and some retail.

Notable Features

- An **overpass** takes walkers above the interstate highway, while clever conversion of a culvert provides an **underpass**.
- The Snyderville Basin **Field House** provides playgrounds, indoor golf and batting cages, a track, climbing walls, exercise equipment, and classes. Find more information at basinrecreation.org/.
- See Walk #25 for additional information about the **Swaner Preserve** Ecocenter. Additional **trails** are available from the Spring Creek Trailhead, a detour from this route.
- Dining and shopping options are available.

Directions:

- Take the **bus** to or **park** at the east end of the Tanger Outlets Mall near the "moose" entrance on Landmark Drive. Find a paved path behind the stores on the SE end of the mall.
- Turn right onto this path and follow it as it bends left and arrives at an elevated bridge over Route 80. Proceed from the bridge straight onto a sidewalk that borders Rasmussen Road. Continue SE along this frontage road and pass three intersections. The third one is Glenwild Drive. (A left turn onto Glenwild enables a detour to the Spring Creek Trailhead with a map and access to additional trails through the nature preserve.)

* Cross Glenwild Drive and turn right to carefully cross Rasmussen Road. Immediately to the left find a footpath to an underpass. Enter the tunnel and exit near the Basin Recreation (Snyderville) Field House.
* Bear left around the field house and find a sign for the 224-Connector Trail. Follow this trail that briefly borders the Swaner Nature Preserve and then intersects with the Newpark Town Plaza, (see Walk #25).
* Cross the plaza to Newpark Boulevard. Continue west on Newpark and shortly before it ends, find a path to the left bordering West Redstone Avenue.
* Turn left onto this path and turn right at an intersecting path that takes you to a tunnel under Route 224. Continue straight out of the tunnel onto a paved path that ends at the Olympic Parkway.
* Carefully cross the Olympic Parkway and turn right, following around a traffic circle to a sidewalk on the west side of Landmark Drive. Pass more shopping, a hotel and restaurants and this sidewalk will deliver you back to the entrance to the outlets mall, **bus** stop and **parking**.

Route Summary:

» Start on a paved trail behind the stores at the SE end of the Tanger Outlets Mall.
» Take this trail over the highway and continue straight on the sidewalk along Rasmussen Road on the east side of Route 80.
» Cross Glenwild Drive and immediately cross Rasmussen Road. Look for a foot path to your left.
» Follow the footpath under the highway and bear left around the Field House when you exit the tunnel.
» Take the 224-Connector Trail a short way to the Newpark Town Plaza. Cross the plaza to Newpark Boulevard and proceed to near its end where there's a trail to the left, bordering West Redstone Avenue.
» Turn left on this trail and right at the next trail to arrive at a tunnel.
» Cross under Route 224 and proceed straight. Continue until this trail ends at the Olympic Parkway.
» Cross the Olympic Parkway and turn right onto the sidewalk that follows around the traffic circle and along Landmark Drive back to the outlets mall.

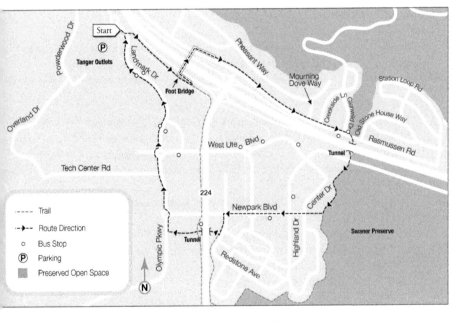

#26 Over and Under Kimball Junction

#27 The Canyons - Sun Peak

Description: This route takes you past some of the amenities of The Canyons side of Park City Mountain Resort, and the adjoining Sun Peak neighborhood with its enviable scenery, trails, and properties.

Mountains provide the backdrop for the Canyons Golf Course.

Distance: 3.0 miles (4.8 km)
Elevation Gain: 272 feet (83 m)
Peak Elevation: 6,804 feet (2,073 m)
Difficulty: DIFFICULT due to a long ascent the first half.
Surface: All paved roads.
Cautions: Vehicular traffic.
Restrooms are not available along this route but may be found if you detour to the resorts and plaza at the base of the ski slopes.

Notable Features:

- The **cabriolet** is an aerial transport system from the parking area alongside of Route 224, to the Canyons Village at the north base of Park City Mountain Resort. It's a **free** ride, but operates only during peak times.
- A seasonal **Farmers' Market** is traditionally held on Wednesdays in the lower parking lot of the Canyons.
- Sharing terrain with ski trails, the Canyons **Golf Course** has dramatic elevations and is as challenging as it is gorgeous.
- Dining and spa services may be available at hotels along this route, or by detour to the Canyons Village. Expect crowds when there's a concert.
- Besides golf, summer activities at The Canyons might include gondola rides, mountain lake fishing, pedal boats, horseback riding, alpine disc golf, a bike park, zip lines, and mountain biking and **hiking**.
- Highly recommended is a short detour to the **Snyderville Pioneer Cemetery**, located on prime real estate between handsome homes. In 1850, Samuel Snyder paid Parley Pratt a yoke of oxen for this mountain plateau, and built a homestead on this knoll.
- This route takes you past trailheads for

The tender ages inscribed on grave markers reveal the hardships of pioneer life.

connecting trails.

Notice local streets with names like "Mahre Drive", "Kidd Circle", and "Picabo Street" honor renowned American skiers.

Directions:

* **Drivers** turn west off of Rt. 224 onto Canyons Drive. Follow around a traffic circle to parking, where there's also a **bus** stop.
* Walk west on Canyons Drive back to the traffic circle.
* Turn right onto Frostwood Drive and continue to another circle.
* Bear right onto Cooper Lane.
* Turn left onto Sunpeak Drive.
* Turn left onto Bear Hollow Drive and continue uphill.
* At the third right corner, turn right onto Mahre Drive, a horseshoe.
* To detour to the cemetery, take the 4th left turn off of Maher Drive, Roffe Road. Proceed up a short hill to a cul-de-sac. The cemetery is on the left. Upon return to Mahre Drive, turn left and proceed to the intersection with Bear Hollow Drive.
* Turn right onto Bear Hollow Drive.
* Turn left onto Sun Peak Drive.
* Turn right onto Cooper Lane, which ends at a traffic circle.
* Bear left onto Frostwood Drive and proceed to another circle.
* Bear left onto Canyons Drive to return to the **parking** or **bus** stop.

Route Summary:

» From the lower parking and bus stop at the Canyons Resort proceed to the traffic circle.
» Turn right onto Frostwood Drive.
» Bear right onto Cooper Lane.
» Turn left onto Bear Hollow Drive.
» Turn right onto Mahre Drive and loop around back to Bear Hollow.
» Turn right onto Bear Hollow Drive.
» Turn left onto Sun Peak Drive.
» Turn right onto Cooper Lane and follow it to a traffic circle.
» Bear left onto Frostwood Drive and proceed to another circle.
» Turn left onto Canyons Drive to return to start.

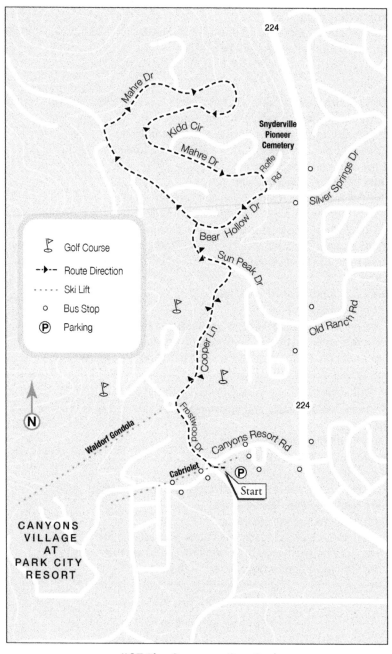

224

Mahre Dr

Kidd Cir

Snyderville
Pioneer
Cemetery

Mahre Dr

Roffe Rd

Silver Springs Dr

Bear Hollow Dr

Sun Peak Dr

Golf Course

Route Direction

Ski Lift

Bus Stop

P Parking

Old Ranch Rd

Cooper Ln

N

224

Frostwood Dr

Waldorf Gondola

Canyons Resort Rd

Cabriolet

P

Start

CANYONS
VILLAGE
AT
PARK CITY
RESORT

#27 The Canyons - Sun Peak

#28 Bear Hollow - Olympic Park

Description: This challenging route provides awesome views and a tour of the Utah Olympic Park where 14 medal competitions took place in 2002. You can make this difficult walk easy by taking the free bus from the Visitor Center to the Olympic Park Museums, and another free bus to the top of the Olympic Park. Then walk downhill the rest of the way.

The most exhilarating show in town is watching aerialists train by skiing off of ramps into a pool.

Distance: 7 miles (11.3 km), but 3 miles (1.8 km) if you take the buses.
Elevation Gain: 892 feet (272 m) if you walk
Peak Elevation: 7,328 feet (2,234 m)
Difficulty: DIFFICULT. This is the most demanding walk in the book due to its length and elevation gain, though switchbacks help a lot.
Surface: All paved roads but with narrow shoulders
Cautions: Vehicular traffic. Possibly, falling rocks along ridges.
Restrooms are available in the Visitor's Center and park museums.

Notable Features:

- Enjoy views of the Canyons Golf Course, Silver Springs lakes, and the Uinta Mountains to the southeast, the tallest east-west chain of mountains in the U.S.A. and the tallest to have not had recent glacial coverage.
- Amicable goats and chickens might greet you at **Bill White Farms** along the **Millennial Trail**. One of the farm buildings was salvaged from the brothel of Mother Urban (see page 12). Woods along the way shelter **wildlife**.
- This route borders the bobsled and luge/skeleton tracks in the 387-acre **Olympic Park** where there are also all-season training facilities for ski jumping. **Guided tours** and lessons are available. The Olympic Park also offers **trails,** bobsled rides, zip line rides, adventure courses, training camps, an obstacle course, a free chairlift ride at peak times, and dining and shopping.
- Enjoy **free admission** to the Alf Engen Ski History Museum and the George Eccles 2002 Olympic Winter Games Museum. Exhibits include virtual chairlift, ramp jumping, and avalanche experiences.
- Even if you don't want to do the big Bear Hollow walk, the walk up Olympic Parkway to the museums is worth the effort. You can also drive up, park at the museums and have an Olympic experience without walking. Additional information about Olympic Park is available at utaholympiclegacy.org.

Directions:

* Take the **bus** to or **park** at the Visitor Center on the NW corner of Route 224 and Newpark Boulevard.

* For the easy route, inquire in the Park City Visitor Center about free **bus** service. If you take a bus to the park top, you can walk this route in reverse and cut out 4 miles (6.4 km). Pass through a pedestrian gate at the park top onto Bear Hollow Road and walk down to Route 224. Turn left onto the Millennial Trail to walk along 224 to return to start.

* If you're doing the big walk, from the Visitor's Center, cross Newpark Boulevard and proceed south on the paved Millennial Trail along Rt. 224, about 1.9 miles (3.1 km) to Bear Hollow Drive.

* Turn right onto Bear Hollow and continue west, climbing for approximately 2 miles (3.2 km) to the gate at the top of the Olympic Park. Find a pedestrian entry around the gate and for approximately 3 miles (4.8 km), descend along the Olympic Parkway.

* Upon exiting the park, just before a traffic circle, turn right onto the paved Millennial Trail and proceed east to the Visitor Center, **parking** and the **bus** stop.

Route Summary:

» Walkers should start at the bus stop or parking area at the Visitor Center on Rt 224 and Newpark Boulevard, the Olympic Parkway.

» Cross Olympic Parkway at the traffic light and find the paved Millennial Trail along Rt. 224. Proceed south on this trail to Bear Hollow Drive.

» Turn right onto Bear Hollow Drive and ascend 2 miles.

» Enter the Olympic Park through a gate and descend on the Olympic Parkway to exit the park.

» Once out of the park, turn right onto the Millennial Trail before a traffic circle to return to start.

» Bus riders to the top of the Olympic Park Highway can exit the park through gate to Bear Hollow Road, and descend for 2 miles. Bear Hollow will intersect with the Millennial trail just west of Route 224.

» Turn left onto the Millennial Trail and follow it north to the Visitor Center, parking and the bus stop, about 2 miles (1.2 km).

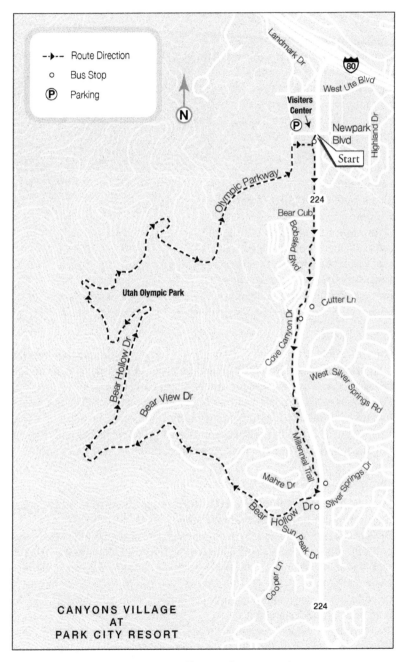

#28 Bear Hollow - Olympic Park

#29 Trailside Park

Description: Trailside Park is a 63-acre community park that provides multiple recreational amenities including several walking routes. Two different loops are described here.

Biking off of ramps in Trailside Park is one more way to get big air. Photo by Ken Hurwitz MD

Distance: A shorter walk is 0.65 miles (1.05 km) and a longer route is 1.12 miles (1.8 km).
Elevation Gain: 59 feet (18 m) for the short walk and 98 feet (30 m) for the longer one.
Peak Elevation: 6,671 feet (2,033 m).
Difficulty: EASY on gently inclined trails.
Surface: Paved black top and some dirt single-track
Cautions: Cyclists, equestrians, skiers
Restrooms are available in buildings on the west side of Trailside Park.

Notable Features:

* The park offers sports fields and courts, playgrounds, off-leash dog-parks, a one-mile **off-leash dog trail**, picnic areas and a **skateboard park**. A **technical skills bike park** can provide thrills for spectators as well as cyclists.
* This walk is easily combined with walk #30 Mountain Ranch Estates. Connections to multiple **trails** including the Round Valley Trail System are accessible from this park. Some trails lead to private property, so become familiar with the trail system if you walk beyond the park. Consult mountaintrails.org/ for maps.

Directions (Route Summary):

* Multiple **bus** stops along Trailside Drive give easy access to Trailside Park, across the street from Trailside Elementary School.
* **Drivers** can access the park by exiting westbound at the Silver Creek interchange on Route 40 to Silver Summit Parkway, or from Old Ranch Road just south of Highland Drive. Parking in the lower Trailside Park lot alongside Trailside Drive gives access to several trails. Alternately, you can go further south on Trailside Drive to the upper parking lot, accessible from Silver Summit Parkway. Parking here accesses additional trails.
* Trails around the park perimeter are easy to follow as they encircle venues within the park. Maps #29 and #30 show additional trail options.

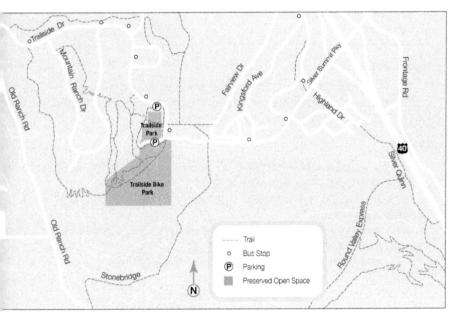

#29 Trailside Park

#30 Mountain Ranch Estates

Description: This road loop provides great exercise and scenery in one of the premier neighborhoods of the Snyderville Basin.

Distance: 2.4 miles (3.8 km)
Elevation Gain: 269 feet (82 m)
Peak Elevation: 6,689 feet (2,039 m)
Difficulty: INTERMEDIATE due to a long ascent
Surface: Sidewalks and paved roads
Cautions: Minimal vehicular and/or cyclist traffic
Restrooms are not available along this route but can be found along the western path through Trailside Park.

As titled, this neighborhood features estates, ranches and mountain views.

Notable Features:

- This walk provides panoramic **views** of terrain all around the basin.
- There's an off-road **trail connection** from this neighborhood that takes you back to Trailside Park to combine with walk #29.

Directions:

- The **bus** stops on Trailside Drive across the street from the west corner of Mountain Ranch Drive. Cross the street to begin.
- For **drivers**, parking is available in the lower parking lot of Trailside Park as described in Walk #29.
- Walk west on Trailside Drive, pass the first corner and turn left at the second corner named Mountain Ranch Drive.
- Proceed around the horseshoe loop back to Trailside Drive.
- Turn right going east on Trailside Drive back to the **parking** lot at Trailside Park, or to one of several bus stops along Trailside Drive.

Route Summary:

- » Start at Trailside Park or the bus stop right across the street from Mountain Ranch Drive.
- » Turn left onto the west corner of Mountain Ranch Drive.
- » Follow the road around the horseshoe back to Trailside Drive.
- » Cross Trailside to the bus stop, or turn right to return to parking.

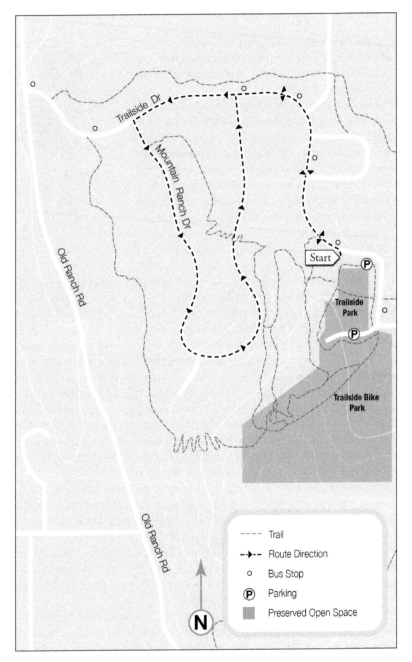

#30 Mountain Ranch Estates

~The ABCs of Walking~

If you hold a newborn infant by her torso and brush the tops of her feet against the edge of a table, a tiny foot will try to step up onto the table. A **stepping reflex** is a sign of neurologic integrity.

If you place your finger against a newborn's palms or soles, their fingers or toes will curl around your finger. Biologists believe grasping and stepping reflexes are instinctive because our evolutionary ancestors lived in trees. Nimble hands and feet, and shoulders that fully rotate, enabled these primates to step and swing from branch to branch to escape predators climbing up trees. Newborns probably relied on grasping hands and feet to cling to their mother's fur as she maneuvered from high to low branches to escape raptors attacking from above.

Newborn humans show a stepping reflex long before they are able to walk.

If you've ever watched a human infant start to walk by holding onto furniture, you'll have observed that feet know what to do well before the brain masters balance. But as soon as that baby finds his balance, he's a walker. How remarkable that healthy people are programmed to know how to walk without ever having to think about the complicated sensory and motor coordination this activity requires. Conversely, someone recovering from a stroke or trying to master use of a prosthetic leg, may need intense training and practice to relearn how to alternately lift and lower their feet, while balancing upright and moving forward.

In normal walking, all of the muscles of the buttocks, legs and feet are active. The back muscles are engaged to prevent falling forward while contracted abdominal muscles prevent falling backwards. Walking uphill gives the glutes and hamstrings extra exercise; walking downhill increases use of the quads and abs. The natural swing of unrestricted arms activates the upper body. More than 200 muscles are involved in walking, including some 40 muscles in each foot and leg. Walking also involves coordination of multiple joints, especially the hips, knees and ankles. Just try to walk without bending your knees or ankles to appreciate this.

There are several differences between walking and running, but the primary distinction is that a walker always has at least one foot on the ground, while the runner is briefly airborne with each step. A race walker would be disqualified from competition if ever airborne during the race.

The difference between "walking" and "hiking" is semantic. Some English speaking cultures define a hike as a longer-than-typical walk. In American culture, "hiking" has come to mean walking in a natural setting, while "walking" is more often applied to getting around town on foot. Physically, they are the same activity and only the environment is changed.

There are a variety of walking "methods" or purposes, including leisure walking, fitness walking, and race walking. **Race walking** was a major spectator sport in Europe and the U.S.A. in the late 19th century. Race walking continues to be an Olympic sport, but it is so difficult that even competitive runners rather not participate. **Fitness walking** requires training beyond the scope of this book, but borrowing from fitness walking, here's how to improve the efficiency of **leisure walking**.

Keep your **shoulders** and **neck relaxed**. Avoid the tendency to shrug or keep hands in pockets when it's cold. Hoods, hats, scarves, facemasks and/or gloves are better than scrunching your shoulders.

Let your arms swing naturally from the shoulders and keep your hands relaxed. You can increase your walking speed by increasing the speed of your arm swing, but swinging arms too wildly can slow you down. Fitness and race walkers keep elbows flexed about 90 degrees and pump their arms to increase speed and efficiency. Serious walkers do not carry or wear anything that restricts or burdens the **free swing of arms**.

Keep your torso upright. Leaning backward or forward reduces efficiency. Some people tend to bend forward at the waist when they are walking up steep hills, but that's counterintuitive. You'll be more efficient and fatigue less easily by keeping your head and **torso upright**, leaning slightly forward at the ankles, and taking shorter than normal steps.

Fitness and race walkers allow their hips to roll back and forth, creating some twist of the waist. Restricted hip movement impairs speed.

Walk heel to toe, avoiding a flatfooted gait. Push harder with the balls of your feet rather than taking bigger steps to increase speed. Bigger steps overwork muscles and slow you. Smaller steps conserve energy.

Retro walking (walking backwards) is popular in some parts of Asia. Many people find it restful to walk backwards for a few paces on a long uphill climb. Research suggests that walking backwards may have some musculoskeletal, cardiovascular and cognitive benefits. Besides the issue of needing a rear view mirror, retro walking in a safe environment may add some variety and fun to your walking routine.

Meditative walking promotes mental and bodily awareness. You could also call this guided imagery, mindful walking, or "woo-woo walking," but regardless of what you call it, it's interesting to try. One exercise, that you first have to read about in its entirety, is to start a walk by standing still with your weight balanced evenly on both feet. With closed eyes feel the ground, then feel your feet, then your legs, then knees, and hips, and continue up your torso. Feel your arms and hands, and then shoulders, neck and head. Then feel the air around you.

With eyes still closed, put one hand on your chest and one on your belly. Inhale in such a way that the hand on your belly rises instead of the hand on your chest. This is called abdominal breathing and it is a recognized medical treatment for hyperventilation, anxiety, and other medical conditions.

Still with eyes closed, imagine that the air you have inhaled is energy that becomes a small ball of light in your brain. Now imagine that you can direct that ball of light slowly down through your torso until it is in your center of gravity, about two inches (five cm) behind and three fingers below your navel.

Focusing on the ball of light, open your eyes and start walking. Walk at whatever pace is comfortable but walk smoothly to keep the ball of light balanced in your center. Extend your head towards the sky and feel the ground beneath you, keeping your focus on the ball of light. You should feel upright, grounded, centered, and relaxed, except for the energy field surrounding the ball of light. You may feel lighter.

While you are walking you will observe things or beings in your environment. Instead of letting them hijack your thoughts, imagine those beings or things emitting energy that you can capture with your eyes. Then, methodically, draw that energy down into your ball of light, and feel that energy flow though your moving body. Do the same with extraneous thoughts. Use your mind to transform all thoughts, sensations, and observations into energy that fuels the ball of light and the motion of walking. If a technique such as this is practiced, it can become automatic, enabling the walker to relieve tension and improve mental discipline and awareness of bodily sensation and the environment.

~Feet and Footwear: The Walker's Essential Tools~

Feet deserve a lot of respect. Those chilly little pancakes at the ends of your legs support a large moving body and whatever other weights you carry. Your feet are the body parts that do the most work in spite of having the least efficient blood supply and flimsy architecture. Sufferers of foot problems should give their feet the best help available.

FOOT BASICS

If you walk across a brown paper bag with wet bare feet, your footprints should demonstrate your foot type. A high-arched foot shows a narrow footprint while flat feet (low-arched) make a wide impression. Optimal foot structure leaves a parabolic shaped footprint.

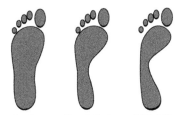

Flat Foot   Normal Foot   High Arch

Knowing your footprint type can guide shoe selection.

A look in the mirror can show your ankle alignment, though it is best seen when you walk. Ankles that tilt or roll inward (**pronate)** are common, as are ankles that tilt or roll outward (**supinate**).

Some degree of ankle pronation and supination is involved in normal walking. As the foot lands on the heel and rocks on to the forefoot for push off with the big toe, it rolls from the inside to the outside and then back to the inside. Young children often look pronated, or "duck-footed" when they first start to walk, but this usually self corrects with maturation. If a young child persistently duck walks, or walks on just their toes, pediatric evaluation is recommended.

Sometimes, what appears to be ankle-tilting, results from asymmetry of the bones above the ankle. If you've just looked at your ankles in the mirror, perhaps

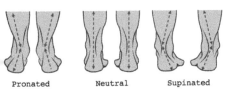

Pronated   Neutral   Supinated

Are you pronated, supinated or just lucky? It depends on your ankles.

you noticed that your legs are not an exact match. Most people have a minor leg length discrepancy. One clue is that when standing, you tend to stand on the shorter leg. If you stood up straight on the longer leg, your short leg would dangle. Another clue is that the waistband of your pants tilts towards your shorter side.

Have an observer look at the backs of your knees to see if the creases line up. Perhaps the creases between the buttocks and the backs of the thighs are at different heights. Putting your hands on your hips while you are standing and then sitting might demonstrate that your hipbones are not the same height.

Did you mirror self-exam also reveal asymmetry of the height of your shoulders? It's normal for the shoulder of your dominant hand to sit lower than your other shoulder, which is why shoulder straps on that side may keep slipping down.

It is also normal for the feet to be different in size and shape. Like the differences between the left and right sides of your face, your feet are unlikely to be symmetrical. Some people may have to buy custom shoes or two pairs of shoes in different sizes to make one well-fitted pair.

Unless you have a known skeletal deformity such as scoliosis (excessive curvature of the spine), all of your asymmetry is likely normal. You don't need evaluation of a leg length discrepancy unless you are experiencing back or pelvic pain, or pain of the joints and muscles of the lower extremity. Those with pain should seek consultation with a health care provider with expertise in musculoskeletal conditions, such as a physiatrist (physical medicine) or sports medicine specialist.

Looking at well-worn footwear can also provide information about ankle alignment. People who over-pronate tend to wear out the inside edges of their shoe heels. They might also notice that the body of such shoes bulges out on the big toe side. Those who over-supinate (also referred to as under-pronation) might see more wear on the heels' outside edges, and shoes may bulge out on the little toe side.

Perhaps inspection of well-worn shoes shows that the soles wear out differently on the left and right. That could warrant an orthotic adjustment on only one side, while correcting the unaffected side could cause problems. If you have significant asymmetry of your feet, a skilled orthotic technician may be able to correct some problems with customized inserts.

Lastly with regard to your precious feet, keeping toenails trimmed is important to shoe fit, footwear longevity, and to avoid trauma to the nails. Toenails should be trimmed straight across, but not too short.

SHOES, SHOELACES AND SOCKS

Before discussing the features of appropriate shoes, I want to make it clear that flip-flops or backless sandals are inappropriate for walking. Such footwear causes you to curl your toes and lift your foot and leg higher than normal, overusing muscles in an unnatural way. Backless shoes also increase the risk of ankle sprains, especially on uneven ground. Barefoot walking is not recommended for any of the walks in this book.

Performance athletic footwear is a multibillion-dollar industry and new shoe designs are sometimes genius and other times disastrous. Below are some basic principles to go by; but in spite of all I am going to tell you about the properties of an ideal walking shoe, keep in mind that there is no shoe characteristic more important than fit. The most expensive, lightweight, durable, and most fashionable shoe on the shelf may be inferior to a cheap, ugly shoe that fits you better.

Good walking shoes should provide support across the top, bottom, back, and sides of the feet. They should feel stable if you hop or jump. Well-designed walking shoes may have an ankle collar (extra padding where the back of the shoe molds around the ankle) or an Achilles notch (a cut-out at the top of the back of the shoe to reduce irritation of the Achilles tendon). Most athletic shoes have a heel counter (reinforcement of the material in the back of the shoe) for added foot stability.

Shoes designed specifically for walking differ from running shoes. Walkers need more shoe flexibility at the ball of the foot for smooth push off. Greater flexibility at the front of the shoe puts less stress on the Achilles tendon.

Runners need extra cushioning across the sole of the shoe as they strike the ground with a flat-footed gait and a force two to three times their weight. Walkers strike the ground with their heels and therefore need more cushioning at the heel. However, the heel flange of some running shoes, or excessive cushioning, can decrease walking efficiency.

Some walking shoes have some curve to the profile of their outsole (rocker bottom), to enhance the heel to toe pattern of a walking step. However there's a lack of good data to support this design and some concern that it may impair foot flexibility and balance. Also check the tread of the shoe's outsole. Thick tread with deep indentations may provide extra traction for slick terrain. Cushy tread may also be more comfortable and durable for those who walk a lot on concrete, but an excessively treaded shoe bottom may impede walking efficiency and increase the potential for tripping.

Shoe flexibility: The blue walking shoe on the left bends behind the toes. The pink running shoe on the right flexes further back, closer to the arch.

Having said all of that, **most walkers will do fine in a comfortable running shoe.** While design differences may be significant for long distance or competitive race walkers, for most leisure walkers, running shoes that provide good fit, support and comfort are usually adequate and much easier to find.

Athletic shoes have traditionally had three basic designs: cushioning shoes, stability shoes, and motion control shoes. Research supporting these designs is limited and there's currently debate amongst runners about the value of "minimalist" shoes, which simulate barefoot running. Preliminary data suggests runners in minimalist shoes have a lower injury rate than runners in traditional shoes. Drop heel shoes are also favored by some runners. However runners have a much higher rate of injury than do walkers, so the relevance of this to walking is unclear. Until footwear engineers come up with another theory as to what is truly best, merchants are likely to continue to offer these three designs:

The rear bumper of the flanged pink running shoe on the right can impede walking efficiency.

Cushioning shoes provide the best shock absorption but less arch support. They are recommended for people with high arches whose ankles tend to roll out (pigeon-toed).

Stability or **neutral** shoes may help reduce mild pronation (ankles rolling in) by stiffening the midsole (the layer between the sock liner or insole, and the outsole.)

Motion Control shoes have stiffer heels and straighter shapes to help with excessive pronation. Some shoes try to correct over-pronation by tilting the foot, using extra padding for the insole, or thicker ridges added to the shoe's bottom. Reducing over-pronation can sometimes alleviate problems like plantar fasciitis or shin splints, but improper tilting can cause or aggravate problems.

Choosing Shoes for Your Foot Type			
If Your Foot Type is	Your likely Ankle Alignment Is	Possibly your Old Shoe Features Are	New Shoes Should Probably Be
Wide shape, Low arch, Flat foot, Points out	Over Pronation Ankles roll in, "Duck footed"	Worn out more on the inside heel, shoe body bulges out over the big toe	Motion Control
Parabolic Shape, Normal arch, Points ahead	Ankles line up straight, Neutral foot Position	Evenly worn shoe bottoms	Stability or Neutral
Narrow shape, High arch, Points in	Supination or Under Pronation Ankles roll out "Pigeon toed"	Worn out more on the outside heel, shoe body bulges out over the little toe	Cushioning

After figuring out what type of shoe you are looking for comes the hard part finding the right type of shoe that fits well. It's understandable why a teen might ask a parent to buy them some blue running shoes in size 7. Seeing a hundred styles of shoes on a store wall can be confusing and intimidating. Although there might be knowledgeable athletic shoe fitters in department stores, you are most likely to find well-trained technicians in specialty stores. In Park City, ski boot retailers employ some true foot fitting experts. Unfortunately, some dealers are more interested in unloading a slow-seller than in helping you find the right kind of shoe for your foot type. You might want to call the store before going and ask to make an appointment with their best fitter, or, ask around to find a reputable store and invest the time it takes to treat your feet like the important body parts they are.

Here are some additional **shoe shopping guidelines:**

Shop after a walk when your feet are puffier. Wear the same thickness sock you'll walk in.

The shape of a shoe should look similar to the shape of your foot. Some people have naturally curly feet (metatarsus adductus), and people who tend to supinate may also get a more comfortable fit from a curvier shaped shoe.

Fit is critical. Either too big or too small will cause blisters, calluses or worse. Start try-ons with your bigger or more troubled foot. Try on as many styles as needed to find the ones that truly accommodate your feet. The difference between a shoe that feels okay and one that feels good will be magnified by walking. Never buy shoes that aren't immediately comfortable. Successful "breaking in" is highly unlikely.

Be careful not to mistake a "cushy" feeling for good fit. Pay more attention to the way the shoe feels all around the foot than to just how the foot feels at the interface with the floor.

The **toe box** should have enough room to allow the toes to freely wiggle up and down. You shouldn't feel your toes jamming against the front of the shoe if you walk down an incline. The heel should not slip. If possible, check for **heel slip** while walking up steps.

Although shoe manufacturers engineer **gender** related features into athletic shoes, some women with wide feet will get a better fit in a "man's shoe" and some men with narrow feet might do better in a "woman's shoe". Finding a good fit for small feet in the children's sneaker department is not difficult, but finding a quality shoe is. **Children's** athletic shoes are often designed more for fancy than foot support, although there are pricey exceptions. Parents should consider that children might deny shoe fit problems if they love the style.

A **removable insole** that facilitates shoe hygiene and allows adaptation to custom insoles is desirable.

Make sure there are no nasty seams, bumps, wrinkles or rough spots inside both shoes, especially if shopping in a discount store. High-end bargains may just have cosmetic flaws or be out of style, but maybe they are **cruel shoes** that someone else hastily bought and returned.

Walk back and forth on a **hard surface**; it can feel different than carpet. If you're down to a choice between two styles, walk on a hard surface in each for a few minutes. Wear them around the house for a day if store policy allows return of shoes that haven't been worn outside.

Buy the **lightest** shoes you can. Mesh is lightest and can help alleviate sweaty feet. Waterproof sneakers and hiking boots are also becoming lighter as breathable fabrics evolve.

High top shoes can restrict walking motion. They might reduce the risk of ankle sprains on uneven terrain and provide added support for weak ankles. However, restricted ankle motion might also impede walking efficiency and balance. Most of the walks in this book are on relatively even terrain that should be navigable with **low-top** shoes.

Buy the best shoes you can afford. Your shoes work harder than any thing else in your wardrobe. An investment in good shoes pays you back in comfort, function, and the durability of your musculoskeletal system.

Always **test** new footwear for short distances before taking a long walk. If new shoes feel wonderful after a few walks and you can, buy a second pair before that style is out of stock.

The everyday walker may be less prone to **trouble spots** if they alternate between a few pairs of shoes. Shoe inserts (orthotics) such as heel cups or cushions may help heel or arch pain or heel calluses. Heel lifts can sometimes correct leg length or pelvic discrepancy. Custom shoe inserts may relieve pain on the inside of the knee. Arch supports or metatarsal pads may improve forefoot pain that sometimes occurs because the shoe is too stiff or too flexible at the forefoot for your foot structure, or because the midsole is worn out. Double-sided tape can secure shoe inserts, though frequent realignments may be necessary. Wrongly positioned inserts can do more harm than good.

Shoes wear out every 500-600 miles (805-966 km) or so, depending on your weight, gait, walking surfaces, and shoe design. An old shoe might still look good while the midsole is disintegrating and no longer providing needed support. Replaceable insoles allow inspection of the midsole. If one particular area is wearing out, a custom insole or a different shoe design might help. Worn out shoes can cause increased knee swing with added stress to knee ligaments and the patellar tendon. Replacing worn out shoes may alleviate some problems and prevent others from developing.

Consultation with a health care professional is strongly recommended for persistent or recurring pain of the foot, ankle, leg, knee, hip, pelvis or back during or after walking. Complex foot problems may warrant consultation with specialists in neurology or orthopedics. A podiatrist could help you make decisions about foot problems and footwear if you take your well-worn shoes to a consultation.

How you **lace** your shoes can impact a variety of shoe and foot issues as demonstrated in this picture. Strategic lacing can improve shoe fit, comfort, walking efficiency, and may solve some foot problems.

A shoe with a thread-the-noodle lace system, like the turquoise sneaker in this picture, provides more lacing options than does standard eyelet lacing. Many laces need double knots or they untie and become a safety issue.

Socks may not be part of everyone's wardrobe but they should be. They can have major positive or negative impact on your walk and your shoes' fit, comfort, hygiene, and durability. As with shoes, **fit** is critical. Too large or too small can cause friction. Avoid tube socks that do not conform to the shape of the heel, socks that are tight around the leg, and avoid any socks with prominent seams.

Socks should sit higher on your leg than the top of your shoes. Low cut socks could turn your shoes into ankle-biters and won't protect your ankles or legs from scratchy plants on trails. Long walkers should choose

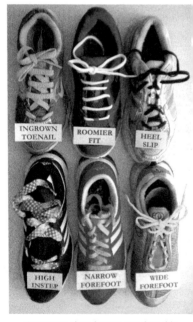

Strategic shoe lacing can handily customize the fit and feel of a shoe.

socks with extra **heel cushioning**.

Avoid wearing worn out socks as thin areas or **holes** can increase friction or pressure, and those areas are usually at the heel or ball of the foot (metatarsal heads) where you most need cushioning. Looking at some well-worn socks gives additional information about your feet and footwear. All socks will eventually "bottom out" but there may be a remedy for why you get holes in certain places.

Wicking fabrics are best. Feet are sweaty organs. An average size foot has about 200,000 sweat glands that under experimental conditions, can produce 28 ounces (828 ml) of perspiration in a week. No wonder the insides of shoes disintegrate! When the skin of the foot becomes moist, it becomes sticky and stretchy, increasing the risk of tears. Cotton socks are not recommended as they tend to absorb sweat, increasing moisture and friction.

Wicking is the capacity of a fiber or knit to transport moisture. Acrylics, polyester, and polypropylene are some fabrics that repel instead of absorb water. When these fibers are woven into a network of channels, the channels become capable of capillary action; like thousands of tiny straws they suck moisture away from the skin. Socks that are suitable for cold weather walking are usually blends of wool and synthetics that have been engineered to increase warmth and reduce moisture and friction. Some people will do better in two thin socks instead of one thicker one.

Avoid wearing new socks for a long walk, if they have not first been washed and **tested** on a short walk. Sweaty feet sufferers and puddle jumpers may want to bring an extra pair of socks along for a long hot or potentially rainy walk. Walking in wet shoes and socks is a great way to get blisters.

Compressive socks may help with conditions such as diabetes or peripheral vascular disease. Compressive hosiery should be professionally prescribed and fitted by a qualified health care provider.

~Other Technology and Gear~

The possibilities are limitless and always evolving, but the purpose of this book is to make walking uncomplicated, so advice is limited to the following:

Google Earth, at earth.google.com allows you to preview all of the walks in Park City, as well as the world. Aerial photography enables visualization of roads, trails, and topography. Bus stops and landmarks are labeled. Using the street level view you can see buildings. The system will plot walking, cycling or driving courses for you. Navigation tools are numerous and this program has traditionally been free. **Open Street Maps** is also free and shows detailed maps at www.openstreetmap. org/#map=13/40.6445/-111.5121. Remember though, any map or satellite image can be outdated due to ongoing changes in roads and trails. Also, trees obscure trails on aerial photos.

Smart phones provide not only a life line for the injured or lost, but maps, a compass, help to identify flowers, birds, etc., and apps for tracking mileage, elevation, calories burned, etc. That's of course when the phone isn't lost or has a low battery; so enjoy your phone but **don't rely on it**. The wise walker knows where they are going ahead of time, and carries information as to who to contact in case of an emergency.

The technologic **advancement** in **textiles** over recent decades is significant. Athletic clothing has become increasingly lightweight, wicking, sun blocking, aerodynamic, and expensive, but discounted brands also benefit from the high tech engineering. While none of this is necessary for a good walk, wearers of old winter long underwear are missing out on the superior comfort, warmth and function provided by contemporary base layers.

Packs for toting water, this book, or other essentials come in a great variety of styles. **Water bottles** should be carefully selected and not made of soft plastic, especially when warm temperatures promote leeching of harmful chemicals out of the plastic and into your beverage**.** Two water bottles, one on each side of a fanny, waist or backpack are better for balance than a single large container.

Writing this book, I was reminded of the famous story of Grandma Gatewood who walked the 2,168 mile (3,489 km) Appalachian Trail alone in 1955, wearing sneakers and carrying a home made duffel bag. You **do not need special gear or clothing** to walk.

For the non-walker, the ideal **all-terrain stroller** has large inflated wheels**,** one in front and two in back, good suspension and shock-absorption, a multi-point harness, reliable brakes, and a locking mechanism to prevent rolling on inclines. **It shouldn't tip** if there are heavy items in the storage bin. If you stroll just on pavement, a less costly model may suffice. Shop in person to check stroller features and the fit for both the rider and pusher. A 25-pound (11.3 kg) tot in a 25-pound stroller can be hard to push uphill.

~Conditioning and Walking With Health Problems~

Healthy people should require no preconditioning to begin a walking program. Start with short walks and if you have the luxury of time, gradually increase the duration of your walks. If like most people, your time is limited, work on gradually increasing your walking pace and/or distance with what time you have. Tackle steeper terrain as tolerated. **Even walking for 20 minutes a few days a week is beneficial.** Add additional walking time by parking further from your destinations and walking whenever possible. You'll probably lose less time doing a brisk walk than seeking a closer parking spot.

Regular walking has been shown to cure some ailments, but even when not curative, appropriate **physical exercise can be therapeutic** for just about every malady known to man. There is a significant amount of research that demonstrates that the prevention and management of these 27 common human afflictions are all improved by regular walking:

Insomnia
Depression
Anxiety
Obesity
Constipation
Irritable bowel
High blood pressure
High cholesterol
Coronary artery disease (angina)
Congestive heart failure
Diabetes
Hypothyroidism
Menstrual cramps
Susceptibility to colds and viruses

Asthma
Emphysema
Low back pain
Joint pain
Arthritis
Osteoporosis
Migraine headache
Chronic fatigue syndrome
Fibromyalgia
Alzheimer's disease
Kidney stones
Breast cancer
Colon cancer

Even for persons who are well conditioned, a walking program should start with an easy pace. For most walkers, it takes about five minutes to get the muscles warmed up, longer in cold temperatures. After warming up, walking pace may be increased to brisk if conditioning is the walker's primary goal. For those who walk briskly, the pace should be slowed down for about five minutes at the end of the walk to let muscles cool down.

As with any unaccustomed exercise, starting to walk can cause **DOMS** (Delayed Onset Muscle Soreness.) That's when it feels great to get out and take a walk on day one, but on day two, the buttocks and/or legs feel achy and tender. With rest, symptoms of DOMS should improve over a few days. Then one can restart walking at a less demanding pace. A physician should be consulted if DOMS is persistent or walking causes pain.

If you are inclined to stretch during or after a walk, bear in mind that stretching is least likely to cause injury if performed when muscles are warm, which is why **stretching before a walk is not necessarily advisable.** Stretching after a walk generally feels good for all those torso muscles that had to contract to keep you upright. The foot, leg, thigh, and gluteal muscles also feel looser if stretched after the walk or a hot shower.

Those walking for leisure may only need to do warm-ups in cold weather and not otherwise worry about these issues. The beauty of walking is the many ways in which it can be done.

Think of the human body as a machine. When levers and pulleys stop moving, rust sets in. Even a long car ride can stiffen the knees. Like cats and dogs, some people aren't ready to get out of bed until they instinctively yawn and stretch out their spines, which often spend the night curled up like macaroni. The more time moving parts sit idle, the more the engine will have strain to start the machine up again. Motion is the oil that keeps the machine functioning. Motion improves bone and muscle strength and lubricates joints by increasing production of joint (synovial) fluid. Walking exercises the lungs, heart and circulatory system, and improves the function of the gut and endocrine glands. Physicians from Hippocrates to cardiologist Paul Dudley White have professed that walking is better treatment for many health conditions than any medicine.

Some medical conditions can be worsened by exercise if performed incorrectly or with excessive frequency or intensity, and some medical conditions require adaptive measures. For example, would-be-walkers with **heart** or **lung disease** or **peripheral vascular disease** should first consult their personal physician. Most of the walks in this book are at **altitudes of 6,500-7,500 feet (1,981-2,286 m)** above sea level. The thinner air of these elevations can cause altitude sickness, and/or aggravate symptoms of chest pain or breathing difficulty in persons with coronary artery disease (angina), emphysema (COPD), asthma, anemia, and other conditions that compromise the body's ability to get enough oxygen. Some persons need to walk at lower altitudes or may require supplemental oxygen under medical supervision.

People with **diabetes** should also seek medical advice before beginning a walking program. Regular walking may result in decreased need for insulin, but increased need for foot care.

Individuals who are very **deconditioned** or who suffer from **neuropathy**, or who have undergone **joint replacement**, may benefit from preconditioning under the supervision of a physical therapist.

Persons prone to acid reflux disease (**GERD**) may avoid aggravation of symptoms by walking with an empty stomach, or by adjusting their medication schedule.

People with **allergies** or **asthma** may need to use an antihistamine or bronchodilator before exercising outdoors. Treadmill walking is an alternative on heavy pollen days.

Individuals who suffer from **chronic fatigue syndrome** or **fibromyalgia**, whose symptoms worsen after exercise, need to embark on a slowly progressive program with built-in recovery periods until tolerance improves.

Persons with **arthritis** may notice some increased joint pain with the start of an exercise program but ultimately, an appropriate walking routine can improve pain and function.

If you are uncertain as to whether walking is or isn't a good idea with respect to your particular medical condition, you should consult with your personal health care provider before starting an exercise program. Assistive devices that will benefit some walkers can range from orthotics and custom shoes, to canes, walkers, cane seats, or electric scooters for periods of rest.

Warning: If walking aggravates your medical condition or causes new symptoms, cessation of walking and consultation with a health care provider is strongly recommended.

~Don't Become The Walking Wounded~

Dehydration is a potentially serious condition that can be readily avoided. Many people who visit Park City blame the altitude for symptoms that result from failure to drink enough water in this high desert climate. Drinking caffeinated or alcoholic beverages that increase water excretion (diuresis, or peeing a lot) can compound inadequate water intake. Walkers who take diuretic medicine (water pills) are also at increased risk for dehydration.

Gradual onset of dehydration causes headache, dizziness, nausea, listlessness, fatigue, constipation and insomnia. Infants and children may show irritability. If dehydration occurs more rapidly, symptoms may include flushing, dry mouth and skin, rapid breathing and heartbeat, and fainting. More severe symptoms include delirium, seizures and heat stroke.

Even though you don't feel like you are perspiring when exercising in Utah's dry air, you are. The sweat evaporates on your skin so quickly that you don't notice it. You also lose water through your lungs; that's the moisture in your breath that enables you to see steam when you exhale on a cold day. You won't see the steam in warm weather, but a brisk walk on a hot day can cause significant respiratory water loss.

Public drinking water sources are limited and taking water along is advisable for all aged people and dogs, especially for longer walks or any length walk in hot weather. If symptoms of dehydration do not improve with drinking a few glasses of water, **acute mountain sickness** might be the cause, and descending to a lower elevation may be therapeutic.

It is possible to drink too much water. A long walk in very hot weather with only water replacement could deplete the body of sodium, causing a serious condition called **hyponatremia** or **salt loss**. Symptoms of low sodium are similar to symptoms of acute dehydration, except the person doesn't feel thirsty and reports having ingested lots of water. Eating something salty constitutes prevention and emergency treatment, but this is a serious condition, especially risky for the brain. Seek immediate medical attention if hyponatremia is suspected.

Chafing can occur when clothing rubs against skin. Inner thighs and armpits can chafe from the rubbing of body parts. In the dry air of Park City, sweat evaporates quickly leaving salt crystals on the skin. The presence of crystals increases the likelihood of skin becoming irritated.

The risk of chafing is reduced by avoiding clothing that is too tight or too loose and by staying well hydrated. Wearing wicking fabrics with minimal seams may help. Application of lubricants at waistbands or bra bands, and or cornstarch applied to sweaty creases is preventive. A variety of lubricants are marketed to athletes for chafing. Even applying some lip balm can help in an emergency.

Blisters occur when there is more acute friction or pressure than the skin can tolerate. The skin responds by making a water cushion between its outer layer (the epidermis) and the underlying dermis where the nerves and blood vessels are. If it's not painful, leave the blister intact, cover it, and fix whatever it is in your shoe that caused it. If it's painful enough to pop, sanitize the area and the pin you pop it with. After the fluid drains, apply an antiseptic and a clean bandage. Check the blister, clean the skin and change the bandage daily. When it's no longer tender, you can trim away the dead skin that protects the newly growing skin.

Calluses are areas of hardened skin that develop to protect underlying soft tissue from repetitive pressure or friction. **Corns** are calluses with dead tissue in their core. Corns are more painful and may require professional management when over-the-counter remedies don't work. Calluses often occur on the heels and balls of the feet as well on the toes. They can be asymptomatic or painful. Calluses develop more readily when bony prominences like bunions compress the skin from the inside, or bad shoes cause exterior pressure. Obesity or having long metatarsals or high arches also increase the risk of bothersome calluses.

If improved footwear does not relieve calluses, they are usually controllable by regular filing. Many products are available for this purpose from pumice stones to battery-powered sanders and devices with multiple sharp blades that require great care to use safely. People lacking the vision or flexibility to attend to their feet should consider professional pedicures. If routine filing does not effectively manage calluses or they become painful or infected, consultation with a health care provider is advisable.

Foot wounds from scratches and scrapes to cuts and punctures all deserve prompt attention. There's a higher risk of infection for foot wounds than for other body parts because sensation and circulation are less robust, feet work really hard, and people tend to not look at their feet. Additionally, feet live in shoes, the insides of which are not too hygienic. The following advice should be considered for the prevention and treatment of foot wounds:

Never continue walking if you become aware of a pebble, shoelace, wrinkled sock, or something else besides your foot in your shoe. Even if it means sitting on the ground, stop walking and fix the problem.

Walkers should check their feet as part of their bathing routine. People with foot neuropathy or diabetes should check their feet after every walk. Even minor scratches or abrasions should be thoroughly cleansed with soap and water and covered with a clean dressing. Applying an antiseptic gives additional protection. Keeping skin wounds covered helps protect from further trauma or infection and hastens healing. Wounds should be cleansed, dried, and re-bandaged every day until healed. **Lacerations** to the bottom of the feet are concerning because if they heal with scar tissue, foot function can be impaired. Big, deep, jagged or dirty cuts of the soles always warrant professional care. If a foot wound does not heal, appears infected, or is associated with increasing pain, immediate medical attention is recommended. Considering that the foot is comprised of 26 bones, 33 joints, 44 tendons, about 100 ligaments, and many fascial planes, foot infections can quickly become complicated and difficult to treat, even for physicians. **Ulcers** of the feet (wounds that do not heal) may require highly specialized care.

Puncture wounds to the bottom of the foot also merit prompt medical attention, especially if the sharp object went through a shoe before entering the skin; and especially if that shoe walked on soil contaminated by industrial or animal waste. If the puncture is deep, scrubbing the surface wont decontaminate it. Such wounds are usually treated with copious irrigation with sterile solutions, and possibly prophylactic antibiotics and a tetanus booster. However, even with proper medical care, puncture wounds can result in bone infection, which usually manifests as pain some weeks after the skin has healed. **Bone infection** (osteomyelitis) is a serious problem that may require surgery and prolonged treatment with intravenous antibiotics.

Ingrown Toenails are an inborn tendency in some unfortunate people whose toenails curl down no matter how carefully they trim them or select footwear. For most people, the nails only grow downward because bad shoes push them that way. Pointy-toed shoes are particularly proficient at pressing on the top and side of the big toe's nail. Cutting nails too short also increases the risk. While ingrown toenail sufferers have traditionally been instructed to cut the nails straight across, there may be some benefit in trimming the nail parabolically, which means allowing the sides of the nail to grow a little longer than the center.

If an ingrowing nail presses deep into soft tissue, it acts like a foreign body, causing inflammation and misery. Emergency management calls for wedging a wisp of clean cotton between the tender skin and the sharp edge of the nail. Soaking the toe in warm water first may help reduce tenderness and soften the nail. It is also less painful to slip the wisp of cotton under the side of the nail than to try to wedge it in by lifting the nail's corner. If elevating the nail does not relieve pain, or if there is drainage, medical attention is the next step. Chronically ingrowing toenails may be managed with surgical removal of the nail or the sides of the nail.

The term **shin "splints"** describes pain in the front of the lower legs, usually due to unaccustomed use. The pain typically involves both legs, increases with activity, and improves with rest. Swelling of muscles, tendons and possibly even bones is the cause. It's important to rest long enough for shin splints to adequately heal. This can take from a few weeks to months, depending on severity, general health, and behavior. Returning to activity too soon can result in stress fractures.

Risk for shin splints is highest in new walkers who are not used to hills, wear inappropriate or worn out shoes, have flat feet, rigid feet, tight heel cords, weak ankles or neuropathy, or who tend to overdo things.

Treatment of shin splints includes avoidance of aggravating activities and footwear, and icing the tender areas a few times a day. If pain persists, cold and/or warm packs should be applied, whichever feels better. Alternating warm and cold packs and/or massage may help. Use of anti-inflammatory medication such as ibuprofen or naproxen should be considered if rest and thermal applications are not helpful after a few days. However, these drugs have significant side effects, especially with prolonged use. They also may interfere with healing and should be avoided if possible. Acetaminophen relieves pain without interfering with healing. Persistent shin splints deserve medical evaluation. Prescription orthotics, physical therapy, or cross training may be able to correct leg alignment problems that sometimes cause shin pain.

Foot drop means the foot isn't effectively or efficiently lifted. A subtle foot drop might appear as a foot that slaps a bit when walking downhill, or leaves a fuzzy footprint in snow. It 's easier to see if only one side is affected. More severe foot drop results in a high stepping gait in which the foot is lifted by increased flexing of the knee and hip.

One of the most common causes of foot drop is having weak stretched-out tendons due to old ankle sprains. A bone spur or scar tissue from prior trauma can also restrict ankle joint motion, or press on the peroneal nerve that controls the muscles that raise the foot. Foot drop may also be caused by spinal problems that impact nerves to the foot, such as spinal stenosis, disc disease, and/or sciatica. Other conditions that affect the foot nerves include diabetic neuropathy and alcohol related neuropathy. Foot drop due to nerve compression has also been associated with a yoga kneeling exercise, the Varjrasana.

Treatment of foot drop depends on cause. While it's often not curable, an ankle-foot-orthosis (AFO), a device that attaches to the leg and goes inside the shoe helps lift the foot. Untreated, foot drop increases the risk of tripping and sustaining injuries, especially on uneven ground.

Foot pain can have multiple causes and is best evaluated by a physician or podiatrist. Inflammation of the plantar fascia (fasciitis), tendonitis, stress fractures, ankle instability, over pronation or supination, nerve impingement in the foot, leg or spine, various forms of arthritis, atrophy of the heel fat pad due to aging, overuse, steroid injections, circulatory problems, and/or plain old bad shoes are some of the conditions that can result in foot pain. The heel is especially vulnerable because it supports 110% of a person's weight with each walking step, and 200% of body weight with running. Some heel pain gets better just by inserting a drugstore heel cushion, and some heel pain can be corrected with customized footwear that compensates for alignment problems. Plantar fasciitis as a cause of heel pain may be difficult to manage, even for health care professionals; but fortunately, it usually improves over a 6-12 month period. Pain of the ball of the foot (metatarsalgia) or the arch, can also have many different causes and is best managed by a foot specialist.

The big toe is referred to as the hallux and disorders of the big joint of the big

toe are common, due largely to heredity and bad shoes. **Bunions (hallux varus)** occur when the big toe points out, the metatarsal points in, and a bony bump on the
inside of the big toe joint slowly enlarges, making it difficult to wear shoes.

The term **hallux limitus** means there is a loss of up and down motion of the
big toe. This condition can result from repetitive use as in the case of golfers who
push off with the big toe to complete their swing, in which case it is referred to as
"golfer's toe". Hallus limitus has also been called "turf toe" because it develops after
an athlete stubs the toe by catching it on a synthetic field. **Hallus rigidus** is advanced
arthritis preventing the big toe joint from being able to bend at all. It's nature's way
of fusing the joint to prevent additional damage. Some people tolerate these hallux
conditions without difficulty, while those with intolerable pain or dysfunction may
need surgery. Foot surgery is a major undertaking that should be deferred if more
conservative options are available.

Ankle sprains occur when tendons and ligaments between the leg and foot are
stretched or torn. Misstepping in a hole or down from a curb are common ways
people overturn their ankles. Most sprains occur when the foot rolls inward, stretching the outside ankle (inversion sprain), but any aspect of the joint can be sprained
depending on what abnormal position the foot gets caught in. Ankles weakened
by previous sprains are at increased risk. Weak ankles may benefit from taping or
bracing, while the value of high top shoes is controversial. Shoes like flip-flops and
stiletto heels are excellent ankle "sprainers". Wearing supportive shoes and paying
attention to where one walks is the best prevention.

Minor sprains may heal without special treatment. Sprains that cause immediate pain and swelling indicate significant tissue damage. If pain is too severe to walk
or there's a suspicion of fracture, walking is best avoided. If you had to get out of
the road without help, options include crawling or using a belt, scarf, or shoelace to
take weight off the ankle joint. As illustrated in the accompanying photo, by looping
a scarf through the shoe laces and pulling the front of the
foot off the ground with hands, walking on the heel may
be possible to at least get to a safe place to sit and call for
help. Getting the front of the foot up may also help take
stress off of the ligaments and tendons. Some practitioners
believe that getting the foot flexed upwards **immediately**
after incurring an ankle sprain can reduce initial symptoms
and recovery time.

Traditionally, care for ankle sprains has been aimed at
reducing swelling by applying ice and compression. While
this approach does reduce initial swelling and pain, it may
undermine nature's healing process over the long term. The
body's natural response to ligament and tendon tears is to
increase blood flow to the areas of injury. Blood contains
specialized white blood cells that scavenge up the debris
of damaged tissue. Increased blood flow also increases the

*Immediately getting
the foot flexed upwards
after an ankle sprain
may improve recovery.*

delivery of nutrition and oxygen to the injured structures and carries away waste. Platelets in blood deliver tissue growth factors. About three days after injury, blood brings cells called fibroblasts to the injury. These specialized cells start the repair process by spinning new collagen. Over subsequent weeks, the collagen will be incorporated into the torn tissue fibers to repair them as best the body can. This is similar to the healing process seen in skin wounds.

Icing and compression reduce blood flow to injured tissue, reducing the delivery of the healing elements that blood contains. Taking anti-inflammatory medicine also impairs the body's own natural repair mechanisms, resulting in delayed and incomplete healing. In other words, inflammation is the first step in the natural healing process. The short-term gain from stopping inflammation may jeopardize the final outcome.

An alternative approach to sprained ankle management favored by some experts includes avoidance of anti-inflammatories, such as aspirin, ibuprofen, naprosyn and numerous prescriptions. Whirlpool treatments or massage may be used to enhance circulation, instead of decreasing it. Walking in an air splint with a cane within the realm of tolerance is also advisable. An air splint allows the normal hinging motion of the ankle to keep the joint from stiffening, but prevents sideways motion, which further stresses the stretched tendons and ligaments.

In severely sprained ankles or those not responsive to conservative treatment, imaging may be needed to rule out fracture, or orthopedic consultation may be advisable. For rupture of soft tissue such as the Achilles tendon, surgery may be necessary.

Hand Swelling is a common walker's complaint. I get baloney fingers on long hot walks, but some people complain of their hands and fingers swelling more in cold weather. There are varied theories as to why this occurs, but for most people, it seems to be a harmless condition that resolves within a few hours after the walk. Stretching the arms upward for a half minute periodically throughout the walk, or performing arm exercises that keep the arms from constantly hanging down may help prevent hand swelling. Hand swelling that persists for more than two days or is painful requires medical attention.

Bees are essential to local agriculture and wildflowers. Most bee species are uninterested in people unless they happen to smell or look like flowers. Bees that nest close to the ground, such as yellow jackets, tend to be more aggressive. Avoid wearing perfume, aftershave, shiny bright jewelry, or clothes with flowers on them. Avoid walking past gardens with children who have dripped sweet juice onto hands or clothes.

If a bee chooses to investigate you, stand still and stay calm. Some beekeepers believe that bees sense fear, which makes them more defensive or aggressive. Staying relaxed may reduce the risk of stings.

Immediate management of a bee sting includes removing the stinger, icing, and taking an antihistamine such as diphenhydramine (Benadryl). It is better to scrape the stinger out of the skin with the edge of a credit card than to pinch and pull it out, as a pinch could cause more venom to be injected. Carry antihistamines and a prescription Epipen (emergency adrenalin shot) if you have a known bee sting allergy, and seek immediate medical attention, even after using an Epipen. The adrenalin in an Epipen is not long acting and more urgent treatment could become necessary very quickly for an allergic person.

Tick born diseases such as Lyme disease are not endemic in Utah, although the tick that transmits Lyme is found within the state. In the 27 years my dogs and I have hiked on Park City trails, I've never seen a tick. Then again, I don't usually go deep into wooded areas or areas with brush or tall grass, nor do my dachshunds whose smooth coats are easy to inspect. Checking yourself, kids and pets for ticks before returning to the car may reduce what little risk there is.

Hopefully, you will never need the information in this chapter.

~Useful Resources~

General Info
Park City Chamber of
Commerce and
Visitor Information Centers
visitparkcity.com
Park City Museum
528 Main Street
435.649.7457
and
Visitor Center
1794 Olympic Parkway
at Kimball Junction
435.658.9616

Other Museums and Libraries
Alf Engen Ski Museum
engenmuseum.org
Olympic Parkway
435.658.4240

Park City Library
parkcitylibrary.org
1255 Park Avenue
435.615.5600

Summit County Library
Kimball Junction Branch
www.thesummitcountylibrary.org
1885 Ute Boulevard
435.615.3900

Swaner Preserve and Ecocenter
of Utah State University
swanerecocenter.org
1258 Center Drive
435.649.1767

Bus Info
Free Park City Transit System
www.parkcity.org/about-us/
transit-bus
435.615.5301

Trail and Open Space Info
Basin Parks-Trails-Recreation
basinrecreation.org

Mountain Trails Foundation
mountaintrails.org
435.649.9619

www.parkcity.org/departments/
open-space-and-trails

Swaner Preserve
swanerecocenter.org
1258 Center Drive
435.649.1767

Summit Land Conservancy
wesaveland.org
435.649.9884

News and Local Info
kpcw radio station
FM 91.7 and on-line
kpcw.org
435.649.9004

The *Park Record* newspaper
parkrecord.com
435.649.4942

pctv1 television station
Various channels and on-line
parkcity.tv
435.649.0045

Avalanche Information
utahavalanchecenter.org
Recorded avalanche
info: 888.999.4019

Entertainment

Egyptian Theater Company
egyptiantheatercompany.org
328 Main Street
435.649.9371

Eccles Center for the
Performing Arts
ecclescenter.org
1750 Kearns Boulevard
435.655.3114

Park City Film Series at
the Jim Santy Auditorium
parkcityfilmseries.com
1255 Park Avenue
435.615.8291

Sundance Institute
Films and festivals
www.sundance.org/festivals/
utah-community

Kimball Art Center
Exhibits and programs
kimballartcenter.org
1401 Kearns Boulevard
435.649.8882

Mountain Town Music
mountaintownmusic.org
435.901.7664

www.parkcitylivemusic.com

www.visitparkcity.com/events/
music-and-concerts

Guided Tours

Deer Valley Historical Hikes
www.deervalley.com/
WhatToDo/Summer
435.649.1000

Park City Museum Historic
Guided Walking Tours
parkcityhistory.org
435.649.7457

Park City Ghost Tours
parkcityghosttours.com
415 Main Street
435.615.7673

Gallery Tour
Park City Gallery Stroll
Free on the last Friday of the
month from 6-9 pm
parkcitygalleryassociation.com

Also

National Ability Center
Sports and Recreation
1000 Ability Way
(Quinn's Junction)
discovernac.org
435.649.3991

Recycle Utah
recycleutah.org
1951 Woodbine Way
435.649.9698

~References~

Find a research library in the Park City Museum at 528 Main Street. Access is available by appointment. Tel: 435.649.7457. The Park City Museum also provides historical information via

- parkcityhistory.org/research/way-we-were-database
- parkcityhistory.org/wp-content/uploads/2012/03/Docent-Manual.pdf
- kpcw.org/term/park-city-history-bits#stream

There is a special section for local history books and documents in the Park City Library, 1255 Park Avenue, 435.615.5600.

The *Park Record* newspaper started publication in 1880. It currently provides weekly articles about Park City history. Find access to its archives at digitalnewspapers. org/newspaper/?paper=Park+Record. The *Park Record* also annually publishes population and economic data in a newspaper supplement called "Milepost".

Some other references of note include:
- extension.usu.edu/agriculture
- historytogo.utah.gov
- www.nps.gov/history
- ocp.hul.harvard.edu - Harvard University Library Open Collections Program
- www.thepeoplehistory.com
- www.utah.com
- utahrails.net
- www.westernmininghistory.com
- www.wikipedia.org
- Elmore, Francis H. *Shrubs and Trees of the Southwest Uplands.* Tucson: Southwest Parks and Monuments Association, 1976.
- Harris, Ron. *Exploring the Geology of Little Cottonwood Canyon, Utah: the Greatest Story Ever Told By Nine Miles of Rock.* Provo, Utah: BYU Press, 2011.
- Livingston Cheryl. "Mother Rachel Urban (1864-1933) Park City's Leading Madam," In *Worth Their Salt: Notable but Often Unnoted Women of Utah,* edited by Colleen Whitney, 122-130. Logan, Utah: Utah State University Press, 1996.
- MacKell, Jan. *Red Light Women of the Rocky Mountains* Albuquerque: University of New Mexico Press, 1962.
- Meyers, Casey. *Walking: A Complete Guide to the Complete Exercise.* New York: Ballantine Books, 2007.

CPSIA information can be obtained
at www.ICGtesting.com
Printed in the USA
FSOW04n1033030617
34973FS